Tough Minds, Tender Hearts

Six Prophets of Social Justice

WILLIAM O. PAULSELL

PAULIST PRESS
New York/Mahwah

Library of Congress Cataloging-in-Publication Data

Paulsell, William O.
    Tough minds, tender hearts : six prophets of social justice / by William O. Paulsell.
        p.   cm.
    Includes bibliographical references.
    Contents: Martin Luther King, Jr.—Simone Weil—Dag Hammarskjöld—Dorothy Day—Dietrich Bonhoeffer—Dom Helder Camara.
    ISBN 0-8091-3184-6
    1. Christian biography.   2. Leadership—Religious aspects—Christianity.   3. Christianity and justice.   4. Social justice.
I. Title.
BR1700.2.P39   1990
270.8'2'0922—dc20
[B]   90-37993
                                                                            CIP

Published by Paulist Press
997 Macarthur Boulevard
Mahwah, New Jersey 07430

Printed and bound in the
United States of America

Contents

INTRODUCTION   v

Chapter I: MARTIN LUTHER KING, JR.   1

Chapter II: SIMONE WEIL   30

Chapter III: DAG HAMMARSKJÖLD   54

Chapter IV: DOROTHY DAY   85

Chapter V: DIETRICH BONHOEFFER   110

Chapter VI: DOM HELDER CAMARA   155

CONCLUSION   186

NOTES   189

Dedicated to

Wayne Harvey Bell

Friend, Pastor, Colleague, Mentor

Acknowledgments

The Publisher gratefully acknowledges the use of selected excerpts from: *Costly Grace* by Eberhard Bethge. Copyright © 1979 by William Collins Sons & Co. Ltd. and Harper & Row, Publishers, Inc. Reprinted by permission of Harper & Row, Publishers, Inc.; *Life Together* by Dietrich Bonhoeffer. Copyright © 1954 by Harper & Row, Publishers, Inc.; *Dag Hammarskjöld: The Statesman and His Faith* by Henry P. Van Dusen. Copyright © 1967 by Henry P. Van Dusen. Reprinted by permission of the publisher; *Where Do We Go from Here* by Martin Luther King, Jr. Copyright © 1967 by Martin Luther King, Jr. Reprinted by permission of Harper & Row, Publishers, Inc.; *Stride Toward Freedom* by Martin Luther King, Jr. Copyright © 1968 by Martin Luther King, Jr. Copyright © renewed 1986 by Coretta Scott King, Dexter King, Martin Luther King III, Yolanda King, and Bernice King. Reprinted by permission of Harper & Row Publishers, Inc.; *Why We Can't Wait* by Martin Luther King, Jr. Copyright © 1963, 1964 by the author. Reprinted by permission of Harper & Row Publishers, Inc.; *The Strength to Love* by Martin Luther King, Jr. Copyright © 1963, 1986 by Coretta Scott King. Reprinted by permission of Harper & Row, Publishers, Inc.; *Letters and Papers from Prison,* Revised, Enlarged Edition, by Dietrich Bonhoeffer. Copyright © 1953, 1967, 1971 by SCM Press, Ltd. Reprinted with permission of Macmillan Publishing Company; *Markings* by Dag Hammarskjöld. Copyright © 1978 by Knopf. Reprinted by permission of Random House, Inc.; *Gravity and Grace* by Simone Weil. Copyright © 1952, 1980 renewed by G.P. Putnam's Sons. Reprinted by permission of The Putnam Publishing Group; *Waiting for God* by Simone Weil. Copyright © 1951, 1979 renewed by G.P. Putnam's Sons. Reprinted by permission of the Putnam Publishing Group. *Through the Gospel with Dom Helder Camara* by Dom Helder Camara. Copyright © 1986 by Orbis Books. Reprinted with permission. *No Rusty Swords* by Dietrich Bonhoeffer. Copyright © 1965. Published by Collins: London. Reprinted with permission; *Charismatic Renewal and Social Action: A Dialogue.* Copyright © 1979. Published by Servant Books. Reprinted with permission. The publisher gratefully acknowledges the use of selected excerpts from issues of *The Catholic Worker,* 55 East Third Street, New York, NY, 10003.

Introduction

As I move about the church, working with laypeople and ministers in retreats and other events, I find a tendency to classify Christians as either activists or pietists. Those with an activist inclination are scornful of those whose religion is characterized by prayer and contemplation and believe that a Christian's energy must be devoted to the resolution of social problems. Those with pietistic inclinations believe that one's personal relationship with God is of primary importance and that social action is no substitute for salvation.

The assumption of this book is that the integration of these two elements is essential to a well-formed Christian life.

That integration has characterized the six people studied here. They were all committed to the development of a world of justice and peace and they were all deeply contemplative. In fact, I believe that their religious study and experience contributed to their work in the world. As the Chilean theologian Segunda Galilea said, "Authentic Christian contemplation . . . transforms contemplatives into prophets and militants into mystics." [1]

Martin Luther King, Jr., Simone Weil, Dag Hammarskjöld, Dorothy Day, Dietrich Bonhoeffer, and Dom Helder Camara were major figures in the world of Christian social action. Most were politically active, all worked for justice and peace, and each had a distinctive spirituality. Four of the six could be classified as martyrs. Three of the six spent time in prison.

Two were Lutherans, two were Roman Catholic, one was Baptist, and one would have considered herself an unbaptized Christian. One devoted his career to civil rights, one to diplomacy, three were primarily concerned with the poor and the unemployed, and one was led by his faith to involvement in an assassination plot. All took enormous risks with their lives, knowing the dangers, but confident of the rightness of their causes.

There is much to be learned from these people, but the point of this study is that all sought deep relationships with God, they had perceptions of a divine presence in their work and they nurtured their activism with prayer and devotion.

Their lives are examples of what happens when action and contemplation are integrated.

During the 1960s and 1970s we saw many social activists at work. Many are now forgotten. I believe that these six people are still remembered and studied today because their activism was not just an expression of a humanistic concern. Their contribution was lasting because of the spiritual base from which they operated. It gave them courage, idealism and a clarity of vision that made the gospel come alive in their work.

CHAPTER I

Martin Luther King, Jr.

MARTIN LUTHER KING, JR. was, without question, the leading American Christian social activist of the 1950s and 1960s. His work produced a revolution in American society, not just in the south, but in the entire nation. He was, however, more than just a reformer. He was a Christian martyr, put to death for his faith while carrying out his ministry.

A brief outline of his life begins with his birth in Atlanta on January 15, 1929, the second child of a Baptist minister. After attending public schools and the Atlanta University Laboratory High School he entered Morehouse College in 1944. Upon graduation in 1948 he enrolled at Crozer Theological Seminary in Chester, Pennsylvania, from which he graduated in 1951, receiving the Plafker Award as the most outstanding student in his class. He was also awarded the J. Lewis Crozer Fellowship to study for a doctor of philosophy degree at a university of his choice.

He chose Boston University where he studied systematic theology and wrote a dissertation on *A Comparison of the Conceptions of God in the Thinking of Paul Tillich and Henry Nelson Weiman* under the direction of L. Harold DeWolf and S. Paul Schilling. During his years at Boston he was also a special student in the philosophy department at Harvard. It was during the Boston stay that he married Coretta Scott of Marion, Alabama.

King was ordained in 1947 at his father's church, Ebenezer Baptist in Atlanta, and served as assistant and later co-pastor with

1

the senior King. In April 1954 he became minister of the Dexter Avenue Baptist Church in Montgomery, Alabama, expecting to spend his time preaching and giving pastoral care to his congregation. However, the next year Rosa Parks, a black woman exhausted from a day's work, refused to obey the bus segregation laws of the city and give up her seat to a white person. Her arrest caused a black boycott of the Montgomery bus system, and King was thrust into the leadership of that effort. Later, he helped organize and became the first president of the Southern Christian Leadership Conference, a post he held the rest of his life. Eventually he returned to Atlanta to resume his position as co-pastor of the Ebenezer Baptist Church.

He was the author of five books and was awarded over two hundred honorary degrees. In 1964 he received the Nobel Peace Prize. On April 4, 1968, he was assassinated on the balcony of a motel in Memphis where he had been leading a protest demonstration for sanitation workers. James Earl Ray was convicted of the murder.

King's work as a civil rights leader is well known. Not only did he lead protests and demonstrations all over the country, he also became a fervent opponent of the war in Vietnam. Less well known, however, was the spiritual base which motivated and directed his work. This side of his life was not often seen on television news programs. Although he was frequently accused of causing violence and public disorder, he was devoted to the principle of nonviolence, a principle which he believed was philosophically sound and an expression of the deepest levels of the Christian ethic. The focus in this chapter is not on the specific social protests which he led, but upon his spirituality and its influence on his work.

SPIRITUAL POWER IN THE UNIVERSE

King's spirituality was grounded in his discernment of a spiritual power at work in the universe, and he understood his own work as an effort to draw on that power. The Montgomery bus boycott could have been explained simply as a protest against injustice. King, however, saw much more than that in it. "There is something about the protest that is suprarational; it cannot be explained without a divine dimension," he wrote in *Stride Toward Freedom*. "Some extra human force labors to create a harmony out of the discord of the universe," he said. "There is a creative power that works to pull down mountains of evil and level hilltops of injustice. God still works through history His wonders to perform. It seems as though God had decided to use Montgomery as the proving ground for the struggle and triumph of freedom and justice in America."[1]

This was the basis for his opposition to communism. He wrote of reading Karl Marx during the Christmas holidays of 1949 while he was a seminary student and how he was repulsed by the rejection of God. "This I could never accept," he wrote, "for as a Christian I believe that there is a creative personal power in this universe who is the ground and essence of all reality—a power that cannot be explained in materialistic terms. History is ultimately guided by spirit, not matter."[2] And, in a sermon called "Our God is Able," King said, "In the long run of history might does not make right and the power of the sword cannot conquer the power of the spirit."[3]

Not only is there a spiritual power at the heart of the universe, King also believed that "the universe is on the side of justice." That is why a person committed to nonviolence could suffer attack without retaliation. "He knows that in his struggle for justice he has cosmic companionship," King said. He admitted that some believers in nonviolence had difficulty believing in a personal God. "But even these persons," he wrote, "believe in the existence of some creative force that works for universal wholeness. Whether we call it an unconscious process, an impersonal Brahman, or a Personal Being of matchless power and infinite love, there is a creative force in this universe that works to bring the disconnected aspects of reality into a harmonious whole."[4]

During the Montgomery bus boycott King attempted to answer a white Methodist minister who said that the church should lead people to God and stay out of "transitory social problems." King answered, "The decision which we must make now is whether we will give our allegiance to outmoded and unjust customs or to the ethical demands of the universe. As Christians we owe our ultimate allegiance to God and His will, rather than to man and his folkways."[5]

In a sermon delivered in Atlanta on Christmas Eve, 1967, King spoke of the Christmas hope. "If there is to be peace on earth and good will toward men, we must finally believe in the ultimate morality of the universe, and believe that all reality hinges on moral foundations."[6]

He prophesied the death of segregation as a principle of law. Its demise represented to King "the inevitable decay of any system based on principles that are not in harmony with the moral laws of the universe. When in future generations men look back upon these turbulent, tension-packed days through which we are passing, they will see God working through history for the salvation of man."[7]

King despaired of the ability of science by itself to improve the condition of people. Something deeper was needed. Physical power that is not controlled by spiritual power will produce only what he called "cosmic doom." He insisted, "We need something more spiritually sustaining and morally controlling than science. It is an instrument which, under the power of God's spirit, may lead man to greater heights of physical security, but apart from God's spirit, science is a deadly weapon that will lead only to deeper chaos."[8]

The power of spiritual force was seen by King in the lives of many people. In his famous "Letter from a Birmingham Jail," he mentioned white ministers who had been dismissed from their churches because of their sympathy with the civil rights movement. "Their witness," he wrote, "has been the spiritual salt that has preserved the true meaning of the gospel in these troubled times."[9] He referred to a statement of Arnold Toynbee in his *Study of History* that blacks may be the ones who will provide the new spiritual dynamic to western civilization that it so desperately needs to survive.[10] King believed that "the spiritual power that the Negro can radiate to the world comes from love, understanding, good will, and nonviolence. It may even be possible for the Negro, through adherence to nonviolence, so to challenge the nations of the world that they will seriously seek an alternative to war and destruction."[11] A naive hope, perhaps, in the light of subsequent history, but King believed that the power of the spirit was enormous.

How does one actually experience this spiritual power that holds the universe together? Such an experience is indescribable. The great mystics flounder when they attempt to explain it. King's discussions of religious experience were also pretty vague. But he did make the effort.

As president of the Montgomery Improvement Association King was asked to speak at a mass meeting on the night of the first day of the boycott. Because of the hectic activity of the day he found himself with only twenty minutes to prepare. "With nothing left but faith in a power whose matchless strength stands over against the frailties and inadequacies of human nature, I turned to God in prayer. My words were brief and simple, asking God to restore my balance and to be with me in a time when I needed His guidance more than ever."[12]

He made his speech, telling his audience that resisting bus segregation was a matter of maintaining self-respect. It was their destiny to bring new meaning into western civilization. He received a standing ovation. "I realized that this speech had evoked more response than any speech or sermon I had ever delivered, and yet it was virtually unprepared. I came to see for the first time what the older preachers meant when they said, 'Open your mouth and God will speak to you.' While I would not let this experience tempt me to overlook the need for continued preparation, it would always remind me that God can transform man's weakness into his glorious opportunity."[13]

In his first book, while attempting to answer the criticisms of a white minister, King wrote, "We too know the Jesus that the minister just referred to. We have had an experience with him, and we believe firmly in the revelation of God in Jesus Christ."[14] What kind of experience did King have with Christ?

One of the most specific descriptions of religious experience in King's writings is found in *Stride Toward Freedom.* He described the various threats which had been made on his life and family because of the bus boycott as well as his growing fears and discouragement. "In this state of exhaustion, when my courage had all but gone, I decided to take my problem to God," he wrote. He sat at the kitchen table in his home and prayed, confessing that he did not know if he could provide the kind of courageous leadership needed. Fear had sapped his energy.

In that act of surrender, something happened. He wrote, "At that moment I experienced the presence of the Divine as I had never experienced Him before. It seems as though I could hear the quiet assurance of an inner voice saying: 'Stand up for righteousness, stand up for truth; and God will be at your side forever.' Almost at once my fears began to go. My uncertainty disappeared. I was ready to face anything."

It was a good thing, for a few days later, while he was out of town, King's home in Montgomery was bombed. "Strangely enough," he said, "I accepted the word of the bombing calmly. My religious experience a few nights before had given me the strength to face it."[15]

Another religious experience occurred in a jail cell. On April 12, 1963, King, along with many others, was arrested in Birmingham for demonstrating in violation of a court injunction. He had agonized over the decision on whether to let himself be arrested. Money was short for bail bonds, and some counseled that he should avoid arrest in order to raise bond money for the others. After a time of soul searching he decided to stand with his friends in an act of civil disobedience; arrest would be inevitable.

He was placed in solitary confinement in the Birmingham jail. When his lawyer, Clarence B. Jones, arrived from New York the next day he had word that Harry Belafonte had raised fifty thousand dollars for bail bonds. King reported that he felt "a profound sense of awe." It was not the money or just that the way had been found out of a hopeless situation. "I was aware of a feeling that had been present all along below the surface of consciousness. . . . I had never been truly in solitary confinement; God's companionship does not stop at the door of a jail cell."[16]

When the first day of bus integration came to Montgomery there was much nervousness, in both black and white sections of town. For several days speakers had urged high school and college students to continue practicing nonviolence. A mimeographed list of "Integrated Bus Suggestions" was passed out all over the city. Among the suggestions were the following:

6. For the first few days try to get on the bus with a friend in whose non-violence you have confidence. You can uphold one another by a glance or a prayer.

7. If another person is being molested, do not arise to go to his defense, but pray for the oppressor and use moral and spiritual force to carry on the struggle for justice.[17]

Although King believed firmly in the necessity and power of prayer he was much concerned about the misuse of prayer. No one should expect God to solve all problems through prayer. This makes God little more than a "cosmic bellhop," King said. Prayer was not to be seen as a substitute for work and intelligence. "I am certain we need to pray for God's help and guidance in this integration struggle, but we are gravely misled if we think the struggle will be won only by prayer. God, who gave us minds for thinking and bodies for working, would defeat his own purpose if he permitted us to obtain through prayer what may come through work and intelligence. Prayer is a marvelous and necessary supplement of our feeble efforts, but it is a dangerous substitute," dangerous because a too heavy reliance on it may weaken one's resolve to work for justice.[18]

One of King's strongest statements on the presence of spiritual power in social reform was in a sermon on "Transformed Nonconformists." Nonconformity has no intrinsic value, he said. In fact, it may be nothing more than exhibitionism. It can be a creative force, however, when it is the result of a transformed life that is characterized by a new outlook. People become new creatures, King believed, when they open their lives to God and have a new birth. This is what frees a person from a cold, hardhearted, and self-righteous kind of nonconformity. It is the religious transformation which prevents a social activist from being "annoyingly rigid and unreasonably impatient." King insisted that "Only through an

7

inner spiritual transformation do we gain the strength to fight vigorously the evils of the world in a humble and loving spirit."[19]

GOD AND EVIL

King did not present a systematic outline of his doctrine of God, although he had explored the subject in his doctoral dissertation. Still, one can glean from his sermons and other writings an understanding of God as a divine power present in human affairs, working to overcome evil. "Religion endows us with the conviction that we are not alone in this vast, uncertain universe," King wrote. "Beneath and above the shifting sands of time, the uncertainties that darken our days, and the vicissitudes that cloud our nights is a wise and loving God. His boundless love supports and contains us as a mighty ocean contains and supports the tiny drops of every wave. With a surging fullness he is forever moving toward us."[20]

King's conception of God had elements of both transcendence and immanence. To say that God is involved in the human struggle does not exhaust the possibilities. "To say that God is person is not to make him a finite object besides other objects or attribute to him the limitations of human personality; it is to take what is finest and noblest in our consciousness and affirm its perfect existence in him," King believed. Nevertheless, in God "there is feeling and will, responsive to the deepest yearnings of the human heart: this God both evokes and answers prayer."[21]

As any social activist must be, King was concerned over the theological problem of evil. In one of his sermons he said, "We admit the reality of evil. Christianity has never dismissed evil as illusory, or an error of the mortal mind. It reckons evil as a force that has objective reality."[22]

But why does a good and loving God allow evil in the world? King had two things to say. First, much of the evil people experience is caused by their own folly and misuse of freedom. That, of course, does not answer all the questions. Second, King suggested that what may appear to be evil may have some purpose that cannot be seen at the moment. He admitted that there was a "penumbra of mystery surrounding God" beyond the human capacity to understand.[23]

King believed that in giving us freedom God "relinquished a measure of his own sovereignty and imposed certain limitations upon himself."[24] God cannot impose a will upon people and at the same time leave them free. Such an action would defeat God's liberating purpose for humanity. People would only be puppets.

Still, King believed that God was at work in the world. "Here on all the roads of life, he is striving in our striving," he said. "As we struggle to defeat the forces of evil, the God of the universe struggles with us. Evil dies on the seashore, not merely because of man's endless struggle against it, but because of God's power to defeat it."[25]

Even so, the question arises, "Why is God so slow in helping people conquer the forces of evil?" One part of the answer for King was that suffering may serve a useful purpose. "By recognizing the necessity of suffering in a righteous cause, we may possibly achieve our humanity's full stature. Our present suffering and our nonviolent struggle to be free may well offer to Western civilization the kind of spiritual dynamic so desperately needed for survival."[26]

Beyond that, King believed that the will of God was at work in everything, even though it may be difficult to see at the time. "Almost anything that happens to us may be woven into the purposes of God. It may lengthen our cords of sympathy. It may break our self-centered pride. The cross, which was willed by wicked men, was woven by God into the tapestry of world redemption."[27]

Furthermore, when we oppose evil, said King, "God gives us the interior resources to bear the burdens and tribulations of life. When we are in the darkness of some oppressive Egypt, God is a light to our path. He imbued us with the strength needed to endure the ordeals of Egypt, and he gives us courage and power to undertake the journey ahead. He is with us not only in the noontimes of fulfilment, but also in the midnight of despair."[28]

King avoided identifying an ideal social order with the kingdom of God. That was one of his criticisms of Walter Rauschenbusch, whom he otherwise admired. "The Kingdom of God," said

King, "may remain a not yet as a universal reality in history." Nevertheless, "in the present it may exist in such isolated forms as in judgment, in personal devotion, and in some group life."[29]

The evil which plagues people's lives was doomed to defeat, King believed. There was a moral law in the world similar to natural law that worked to prevent the triumph of evil. "The Hitlers and Mussolinis have their day, and for a period they may wield great power, spreading themselves like a green bay tree, but soon they are cut down like the grass and wither as the green herb."[30]

In Christian theology it has always been difficult to reconcile the wrath and love of God. King dealt with this in a sermon called "A Tough Mind and a Tender Heart." His point was, "The greatness of our God lies in the fact that he is both toughminded and tenderhearted. He has qualities both of austerity and of gentleness. The Bible, always clear in stressing both attributes of God, expresses his toughmindedness in his justice and wrath and his tenderheartedness in his love and grace. God has two outstretched arms. One is strong enough to surround us with justice, and one is gentle enough to embrace us with grace."[31]

King felt that a God only concerned with justice would be "a cold, passionless despot sitting in some far-off heaven 'contemplating all.' " However, a purely tenderhearted God would be "too soft and sentimental to function when things go wrong and incapable of controlling what he has made." King concluded, "We can be thankful that our God combines in his nature a creative synthesis of love and justice which will lead us through life's dark valleys and into sunlit pathways of hope and fulfilment."[32]

FAITH

Essential to an understanding of King's theology is his concept of faith. In a sermon, "Shattered Dreams," he said that our ability to deal with the hard realities of life depended on the depth of our faith in God. "Genuine faith," he wrote, "imbued us with the conviction that beyond time is a divine spirit and beyond life is Life.

However dismal and catastrophic may be the present circumstances, we know we are not alone, for God dwells with us in life's most confining and oppressive cells."[33]

Nevertheless, for King faith was more than just believing that God exists. It was an act of opening oneself to the power of God. "Moral victory will come," King said, "as God fills man and man opens his life by faith to God. Racial justice . . . will come neither by our frail and often misguided efforts nor by God imposing his will on wayward men, but when enough people open their lives to God and allow him to pour his triumphant, divine energy into their souls."[34]

He explained further, "One cannot remove an evil habit by mere resolution nor by simply calling on God to do the job, but only as he surrenders himself and becomes an instrument of God. We shall be delivered from the accumulated weight of evil only when we permit the energy of God to come into our souls."[35] This, for King, was what it meant to become a new person in Christ.

However, faith did not mean expecting God to do everything. "We must never feel that God will, through some breath-taking miracle or a wave of the hand, cast evil out of the world. As long as we believe this we will pray unanswerable prayers and ask God to do things he will never do. The belief that God will do everything for man is as untenable as the belief that man can do everything for himself. It, too, is based on a lack of faith. We must learn that to expect God to do everything while we do nothing is not faith, but superstition." What was required to produce change was the combination of the love of God freely given and human obedience and receptivity. "The principle which opens the door for God to work through man is faith."[36]

King described an important incident in the Montgomery bus boycott. The city was attempting to enjoin the operation of the car pool the blacks had organized to provide transportation for the boycotters. If it succeeded the boycott might well collapse. At a mass meeting King attempted to explain the situation to a discouraged audience. He concluded his speech, "We have moved all these months in the daring faith that God is with us in our struggle. Many experiences of days gone by have vindicated that faith in a marvelous way. Tonight we must believe that a way will be made out of no way."[37] But he sensed a deep pessimism in the black community and felt profoundly discouraged.

The next day at a recess in a hearing on the use of car pools, the word came that the Supreme Court had ruled bus segregation unconstitutional in Montgomery. From the back of the courtroom someone shouted, "God Almighty has spoken from Washington." It would be easy to see the timing of this ruling as coincidental, but King believed that it was the result of the power of faith.[38]

There were times, King knew and experienced, when it was difficult to have faith. Only the belief that God is good and just makes faith possible. But when one has faith, he wrote, "he knows that the contradictions of life are neither final nor ultimate. He can walk through the dark night with the radiant conviction that all things work together for good for those that love God. Even the most starless midnight may herald the dawn of some great fulfilment."[39]

INTELLECTUAL INFLUENCES

The public image of Martin Luther King, Jr. has been that of a social activist and a preacher. Little noticed by most people was Martin Luther King, Jr. the intellectual. A reading of his doctoral dissertation at Boston reveals his potential as a theologian. Indeed, had he lived in other times under other circumstances his vocation might have been that of a black intellectual and theologian.

A major factor in the development of King's ideas on Christian social reform was the doctrine of human nature that King came to believe. In several of his books he described his intellectual pilgrimage which finally led to his understanding of human nature.

He had no use for what he called "soft-minded" religious thinking or for any action of the church which might inhibit the search for truth. He saw the benefits of modern advances in biblical scholarship and realized that many people were threatened by it. "The historical-philological criticism of the Bible is considered by the softminded as blasphemous, and reason is often looked upon as the exercise of a corrupt faculty. Soft-minded persons have revised the Beatitudes to read, 'Blessed are the pure in ignorance, for they shall see God.' "[40] In a sermon, "Love in Action," he reminded his audience, "We are commanded to love God, not only with our hearts and souls, but also with our minds. Over and again the Bible reminds us of the danger of zeal without knowledge and sincerity without intelligence." Jesus was crucified, he said, because of stupidity. "They know not what they do." Most human problems, King believed, were caused by stupidity. "One day we will learn that the heart can never be totally right if the head is totally wrong. The call for intelligence is a call for openmindedness, sound judgment, and love for truth. It is a call for men to rise above the stagnation of closemindedness and the paralysis of gullibility."[41]

Like most southerners in his denomination, King was raised in a strict fundamentalist tradition. As he moved through college and seminary and on to graduate school he was sometimes shocked by what to him were new ideas. However, he said that the pilgrimage stimulated him and awakened him from his dogmatic slumber. Liberalism, he said, "provided me with an intellectual satisfaction that I had never found in fundamentalism. I became so enamoured of the insights of liberalism that I almost fell into the trap of accepting uncritically everything it encompassed. I was absolutely convinced of the natural goodness of man and the natural power of human reason."[42]

There came a time, however, when he began to question certain liberal ideas. While he appreciated liberalism's devotion to the search for truth, its insistence on an open and analytical mind, and its refusal to abandon the best lights of reason, he began to question its understanding of human nature. "The more I observed the tragedies of history and man's shameful inclination to choose the low road, the more I came to see the depths and strength of sin. Moreover, I came to recognize the complexity of man's social involvement and the glaring reality of collective evil. I also came to see that the superficial optimism of liberalism concerning human nature overlooked the fact that reason is darkened by sin."[43]

Among the first books to make a major impression on King at Crozer seminary was Walter Rauschenbusch's *Christianity and the*

Social Crisis. He praised Rauschenbusch for insisting that the gospel deals with the whole person, body and soul, spiritual and material well-being. "It has been my conviction ever since reading Rauschenbusch that any religion which professes to be concerned about the souls of men and is not concerned about the social and economic conditions that scar the soul, is a spiritually moribund religion only waiting to be buried."[44]

After reading Rauschenbusch, King turned to other social philosophers such as Plato, Aristotle, Rousseau, Bentham, Mill, Locke and Marx. He encountered so many new ideas that he almost despaired of the power of love to solve social problems. It might be useful in resolving problems between individuals, but when racial groups and nations were hostile to each other, something more realistic would be needed.

As a corrective to liberalism King turned to neo-orthodox theologians, especially Reinhold Niebuhr, whose works he read during his last year in seminary. "The prophetic and realistic elements in Niebuhr's passionate style and profound thought were appealing to me."[45] Niebuhr made him aware of the complexity of human motives and the existence of sin on every level of human existence. He began to develop a sense of collective evil. "I realized that liberalism had been all too sentimental concerning human nature and that it leaned toward a false idealism." King said that while he still believed in the human capacity for good, Niebuhr helped him realize the human potential for evil.[46]

Still, King felt that neo-orthodoxy was too pessimistic. It was too extreme in stressing that God was unknown, hidden and wholly other. "In its revolt against over-emphasis on the power of reason and liberalism, neo-orthodoxy fell into a mood of antirational and semi-fundamentalism, stressing a narrow uncritical biblicism."[47]

King also wrote of his growing appreciation for existentialism. He studied Kierkegaard, Nietzsche, Jaspers, Heidegger and Sartre. He was especially influenced by Tillich who, said King, "had grasped certain basic truths about man and his condition that could not be overlooked."[48] King was beginning to see that human nature was a much more complicated matter than he had realized.

The teachers King particularly appreciated at Boston were

Dean Walter Muelder, Professors Allen Knight Chalmers, E.S. Brightman and Harold DeWolf, under whom he wrote his dissertation. These men introduced him to personalistic philosophy, "the theory that the clue to the meaning of ultimate reality is found in personality." This outlook developed in King two convictions: "it gave me a metaphysical and philosophical grounding for the idea of a personal God, and it gave me a metaphysical basis for the dignity and worth of all human personality."[49]

Of all the thinkers who influenced King, however, none had a greater impact than Gandhi. While at Crozer, King had begun to despair about the power of love to solve social problems. His entire outlook was changed, however, when he heard Mordecai Johnson, the president of Howard University, speak on Gandhi. King found the message so profound and electrifying that he immediately bought six books on Gandhi's life and ideas. "I had heard of Gandhi, but had never studied him seriously," King wrote. "As I delved deeper into the philosophy of Gandhi my skepticism concerning the power of love gradually diminished, and I came to see for the first time its potency in the area of social reform. Prior to reading Gandhi, I had about concluded that the ethics of Jesus were only effective in individual relationships. But after reading Gandhi, I saw how utterly mistaken I was."[50]

King felt that Gandhi was the first person in history to use Jesus' love ethic as an effective social force on a large scale. "It was in this Gandhian emphasis on love and nonviolence that I discovered the method for social reform that I had been seeking for many months. I came to feel that this was the only morally and practically sound method open to oppressed people in their struggle for freedom."[51]

An essential key to the success of nonviolent resistance to evil is a willingness to suffer, and King was to experience the truth of that many times. However, he believed that unearned suffering had redemptive, educational and transforming power. Among the few quotations from Gandhi in King's writings were these two sentences: "Things of fundamental importance to people are not secured by reason alone, but have to be purchased with suffering. Suffering is infinitely more powerful than the law of the jungle for converting the opponent and opening his ears which are otherwise shut to the voice of reason."[52]

In his enthusiasm for Gandhi's philosophy King was puzzled by Reinhold Niebuhr's rejection of pacificism. "True pacificism," King believed, "is not unrealistic submission to evil power, as Niebuhr contends." Gandhi's writings had convinced King that pacificism was not nonresistance to evil, but a nonviolent form of resistance to evil. True pacifism, said King, is "a courageous confrontation of evil by the power of love, in the faith that it is better to be the recipient of violence than the inflicter of it, since the latter only multiplies violence and bitterness in the universe, while the former may develop a sense of shame in the opponent and thereby bring about a transformation and change of heart."[53]

Still, the influence of Niebuhr was strong on King, and moved him to arrive at what he called "realistic pacifism." For one thing, King felt that pacifism would have greater appeal if it "did not claim to be free from the moral dilemmas that the Christian non-pacifist confronts."[54]

MINISTRY

In 1954 King ended his formal education and moved from Boston to Montgomery. In sorting out all of the various intellectual influences on his mind he developed what he hoped would be a positive social philosophy. One of the most basic ideas in his philosophy was "the conviction that nonviolent resistance was one of the most potent weapons available to oppressed people in their quest for social justice." At that point in his life, however, this was an intellectual, not an existential, conviction. He had no plans for actually putting it into effect. "When I went to Montgomery as a pastor, I had not the slightest idea that I would later become involved in a crisis in which nonviolent resistance would be applicable."[55]

On December 1, 1955, in Montgomery, Alabama, Rosa Parks was returning home from her job at a downtown department store. Weary from the day's work she sat down in seats reserved for white patrons on the bus. Soon every seat in the bus was filled and the driver ordered Mrs. Parks to stand up so a white man could have her seat. She refused and was arrested. Although accused of being planted there by the NAACP, Mrs. Parks was tired and had reached the point where she was not going to suffer the indignity of segregation that day.

The Montgomery blacks were aroused by the action, and, under the leadership of black ministers of several denominations, they decided to boycott the Montgomery bus system until the pattern of segregation was changed. At this point the demands were moderate: blacks should be allowed to take available seats from the back toward the front, whites would take seats from the front toward the back. King was almost immediately thrust into the leadership of the boycott movement where he would face enormous opposition from the city, the local press, the White Citizens Council, white churches and others.

King urged a nonviolent approach, although the terminology had not yet been established. "From the beginning," he wrote, "a basic philosophy guided the movement. This guiding principle has since been referred to variously as nonviolent resistance, noncooperation and passive resistance. But in the first days of the .protest none of these expressions was mentioned: the phrase most often heard was 'Christian love.' It was the Sermon on the Mount, rather than a doctrine of passive resistance, that initially inspired the Negroes of Montgomery to dignified social action."[56]

As the protest unfolded the influence of Gandhi began to assert itself. After the boycott had been in effect for about a week a white woman, sympathetic to the movement, wrote a letter to the editor of the *Montgomery Advertiser* pointing out similarities between the bus protest and Gandhi's work in India. The woman died about a year and a half later, having suffered much abuse from Montgomery whites, but her letter caused Gandhi's name and ideas to become well known in Montgomery as a result of her letter. Nonviolent resistance now emerged as the methodology of the boycott. As King wrote, "Christ furnished the spirit and motivation, while Gandhi furnished the method."[57]

In his weekly speeches at mass meetings of blacks, King repeatedly stressed the impracticality of violence in the struggle to overcome segregation. "To meet hate with retaliatory hate would do nothing but intensify the existence of evil in the universe. Hate begets hate; violence begets violence; toughness begets a greater toughness. We must meet the forces of hate with the power of love; we must meet physical force with soul force. Our aim must never be to defeat or humiliate the white man, but to win his friendship and understanding."[58]

In *Stride Toward Freedom* King listed six basic aspects of nonviolence.[59]

First, King insisted that nonviolent resistance is not a coward's way. It does involve resistance. It is not passive, but is active in its opposition to evil. For the nonviolent resister "his mind and emotions are always active, constantly seeking to persuade his opponent that he is wrong. The method is passive physically, but strongly active spiritually. It is not passive nonresistance to evil, it is active nonviolent resistance to evil."

Second, nonviolence "does not seek to defeat or humiliate the opponent, but to win his friendship and understanding. Boycotts and demonstrations are not ends in themselves; their purpose is simply "to awaken a sense of moral shame in the opponent." Redemption and reconciliation were the goals of such action.

Third, nonviolent resistance is always directed against evil itself rather than the persons who happen to be doing evil. The enemy is evil, not person. King told the Montgomery boycotters, "We are out to defeat injustice and not white persons who may be unjust."

Fourth, the success of a nonviolent campaign requires a commitment to accept suffering without retaliation. Many of the demonstrations King led attracted violence, and the demonstrators suffered at the hands of their tormentors. To accept blows from another without striking back required enormous courage, but this was the heart of the nonviolent method. And, said King, "If going to jail is necessary one enters it as 'a bridegroom enters the bride's chamber.' "

Fifth, nonviolent resistance not only excludes external physical violence, but also avoids doing psychological or internal violence to the spirit. Nonviolent resisters must never become bitter or indulge in hate campaigns. "To retaliate in kind would do nothing but intensify the existence of hate in the universe," said King. "Along the ways of life, someone must have sense enough and morality enough to cut off the chain of hate. This can only be done by projecting the ethic of love to the center of our lives."

Love for an enemy, in this sense, said King, is not "a sentimental or affectionate emotion." He understood the agape love of the gospel as a love "seeking to preserve and create community." It is a kind of love that sacrifices self-interest for the sake of rebuilding broken community. "The cross," he said, "is the eternal expression of the length to which God will go in order to restore broken community." Responding to hate with hate only serves to destroy community. *Agape* love recognizes that to harm one person weakens the entire community.

Sixth, nonviolent resistance, for King, assumed that "the universe is on the side of justice." This is why the resister can accept suffering. The resister has faith in that justice and right will ultimately prevail.

In King's second book, *Why We Can't Wait,* the discussion of nonviolence emphasized a spiritual foundation. "Perhaps even more vital in the Negro's resistance to violence was the force of his deeply rooted spiritual beliefs," King wrote. The leadership of black churches in nonviolent protests could not be attributed just to sociological factors. "The Negro turned his back on force not only because he knew he could not win his freedom through physical force but also because he believed that through physical force he could lose his soul."[60] King noted that early Christian martyrdoms had created a moral offensive that shook the Roman empire. Negroes, he said, were willing to take the same risk if it could affect the social conscience of the nation. Nonviolent resistance required maturity because it represented a break with the deeply ingrained idea that strong self-defense was an expression of American manhood. "It is not simple to adopt the credo that moral force has as much strength and virtue as the capacity to return a physical blow; or that to refrain from hitting back requires more will and bravery than the automatic reflexes of defense."[61]

There was, of course, a practical side to nonviolence. It forced whites to do violence to blacks in the open light of day where the whole world could see. It put on television and in the newspapers the mistreatment of blacks that had heretofore been hidden. Much of the brutality which had been used to keep blacks "in their place" became ineffective when done out in the open. But the price was high. King admitted, "It is true that some demonstrators suffered violence, and that a few paid the extreme penalty of death. They were the martyrs of last summer who laid down their lives to put an end to the brutalizing of thousands who had been beaten and bruised and killed in dark streets and back rooms of sheriff's offices, day in and day out, in hundreds of summers past."[62]

But this was not all there was to it. Everyone who volunteered to help in demonstrations in Birmingham in 1962 had to sign a commitment card that stated:

I will keep the following ten commandments:

1. Meditate daily on the teachings and life of Jesus.
2. Remember always that the nonviolent movement in Birmingham seeks justice and reconciliation—not victory.
3. Walk and talk in the manner of love, for God is love.
4. Pray daily to be used by God in order that all might be free.
5. Sacrifice personal wishes in order that all might be free.
6. Observe with both friend and foe the ordinary rules of courtesy.
7. Seek to perform regular service for others and for the world.
8. Refrain from violence of fist, tongue, or heart.
9. Strive to be in good spiritual and bodily health.
10. Follow the directions of the movement and of the captains of a demonstration.[63]

Chapter Five of *Why We Can't Wait* is King's famous "Letter From a Birmingham Jail." Among other things he attempted to answer the charge that he was an outside agitator. He replied that his critics failed to express any concern for the conditions that made the demonstrations necessary. "Injustice anywhere is a threat to justice everywhere."[64]

In this letter he outlined four basic steps in any nonviolent campaign: (1) collection of the facts to determine whether injustices exist; (2) negotiation; (3) self-purification; (4) direct action. The purpose of the direct action was to create a situation where a community which heretofore has refused to negotiate would have to face the issue. Often this would happen only when there was tension. King affirmed, "I have earnestly opposed violent tension, but there is a type of constructive, non-violent tension which is necessary for growth."[65]

Actually, King pointed out later in the letter that nonviolent demonstrators did not create tension. They simply brought to the surface the hidden tension that already existed. "Like a boil that can never be cured so long as it is covered up but must be opened with all its ugliness to the natural medicines of air and light, injustice must be exposed, with all the tension its exposure creates, to the light of human conscience and the air of national opinion before it can be cured."[66]

King was distressed that he and his associates were being called rabble-rousers and outside agitators when their work was based on spiritual principles and nonviolence. He warned that if white leadership rejected their nonviolent efforts the only realistic alternative would be violence. "The Negro has many pent-up resentments and latent frustrations, and he must release them. So let him march: let him make prayer pilgrimages to the city hall: let him go on freedom rides—and try to understand why he must do so. If his repressed emotions are not released in nonviolent ways, they will seek expression through violence; this is not a threat but a fact of history."[67]

King's fourth book, *Where Do We Go From Here: Chaos or Community?* published in 1967, contained a strong condemnation of black power and black nationalism movements. He reflected on his past efforts, from Montgomery in 1956 to Selma in 1965, and the efforts to keep a nonviolent philosophy in the forefront. As long as there was reasonable hope for change his ideas were respected. But, he said, "When people come to see that in spite of progress their conditions were still insufferable, when they looked out and saw more poverty, more school segregation and more slums, despair began to set in." King said that in all the places he had given speeches, to both white and black audiences, he had thus far only been booed once. That was in a mass meeting in Chicago and his hecklers were young members of the black power movement. He resented their booing, for he had devoted all of his energy, often at great sacrifice, to helping people just like them. But on calmer reflection he realized the reasons for their opposition. "They were now booing because they felt that we were unable to deliver on our promises. They were booing because we had urged them to have faith in people who had too often proved to be unfaithful. They were now hostile because they were watching the dream that they had so readily accepted turn into a frustrating nightmare."[68]

However, King was convinced that revolution simply cannot be sustained by despair. The only thing that keeps a revolution going is hope. Disappointments are inevitable and must be faced, but hope must be maintained. "The only healthy answer lies in one's honest recognition of disappointment even as he still clings to hope, one's acceptance of finite disappointment even while clinging to infinite hope." Self-pity, he said, will lead only to a "self-defeating black paranoia," and believing that one cannot win the struggle for justice will lead to "a black nihilism that seeks disruption for disruption's sake."[69] The only thing to do is accept disappointments and cling to hope.

King was a realist about American politics. He felt, for example, that an effort to elect all black candidates just because they were black was politically unsound and morally unjustifiable. He knew that black politicians could be as opportunistic as white politicians if their constituency is not informed and pressing for social justice. "What is most needed," King believed, "is a coalition of Negroes and liberal whites that will work to make both major parties truly responsive to the needs of the poor."[70]

King spelled out specific objections to the black power movement. First, he said, "In a multiracial society no group can make it alone."[71] It is wrong to assume that other groups rose to power

22

through separatism. Groups like the Irish, for example, allied themselves with political machines and trade unions. Blacks will need constructive alliances with the majority.

Another factor that concerned him was black power's belief in retaliatory violence. "Now the plain, inexorable fact," said King, "is that any attempt of the American Negro to overthrow his oppressor with violence will not work." Furthermore, King believed that no colored nation in the world showed any potential for leading a revolution of international proportions. "The hard cold facts today indicate that the hope of the people of color in the world may well rest on the American Negro and his ability to reform the structure of racist imperialism from within and thereby turn the technology and wealth of the west to the task of liberating the world from want."[72]

King saw the futility of violence in the ghetto riots of the mid-1960s. "One sees screaming youngsters and angry adults fighting hopelessly and aimlessly against impossible odds. Deep down within them you perceive a desire for self-destruction, a suicidal longing. Nowhere have the riots won any concrete improvement such as have the organized protest demonstrations."[73]

Violence, said King, is simply unable to appeal to conscience. Power and morality must work together. Whites feared that if blacks ever did attain power they would seek revenge for the years of injustice and brutality. "The problem with hatred and violence is that they intensify the fears of the white majority and leave them less ashamed of their prejudices toward Negroes. Violence is the antithesis of creativity and wholeness. It destroys community and makes brotherhood impossible."[74]

Violence only multiplied evil and often created what it sought to destroy. "The beauty of nonviolence," King believed, "is that in its own way and in its own time it seeks to break the chain reaction of evil. With a majestic sense of spiritual power, it seeks to elevate truth, beauty and goodness to the throne. Therefore I will continue to follow this method because I think it is the most practically sound and morally excellent way for the Negro to achieve freedom." In fact, he said that if all blacks in America turned to violence as a means of social reform, he would still "choose to be that one lone voice preaching that this is the wrong way." King felt strongly that a nonviolent approach to social change was needed because "a dark, desperate, confused, and sin-sick world waits for this new kind of man and his new kind of power."[75]

CHRIST

What was the place of Jesus Christ in the faith of Martin Luther King, Jr.? Some of his statements about Jesus were very traditional. In speaking of people who feel guilt he said, "We must lead them to Christ who will offer them the fresh bread and forgiveness."[76] His devotion to Christ was indicated in the direction on the Birmingham demonstration commitment card to "meditate daily on the life and teachings of Jesus."[77]

Most statements, however, were more directly related to his reforming goals. For example, in 1958 he wrote: "Racial segregation is a blatant denial of the unity which we have in Christ, for in Christ there is neither Jew nor Gentile, bond nor free, Negro nor white."[78] Almost ten years later, in *Trumpet of Conscience,* he elaborated on this point. "In Christ there is neither male nor female. In Christ there is neither communist nor capitalist. In Christ, somehow, there is neither bond nor free. We are all one in Christ Jesus. And when we truly believe in the sacredness of human personality, we won't exploit people."[79]

In another context King described Jesus as an extremist. He was such an extremist that he called upon people to love their enemies. He was such an extremist that he was crucified. "In that dramatic scene on Calvary's hill three men were crucified. We must never forget that all three were crucified for the same crime—the crime of extremism. Two were extremists for immorality, and thus fell below their environment. The other, Jesus Christ, was an extremist for love, truth and goodness, and thereby rose above his environment. Perhaps the South, the nation and the world are in dire need of creative extremists."[80]

In a sermon on noncomformism he used Jesus as the perfect example. The command to refuse conformity to the values of the world came from "Jesus Christ, the world's most dedicated non-conformist, whose ethical nonconformity still challenges the conscience of mankind."[81]

THE CHURCH

King often complained about the weakness of the church, especially the white church, in overcoming the segregation system. While he held a prophetic view of the church, the reality he faced was often one of timidity and conformity.

In his first book he described the Dexter Avenue Baptist Church in Montgomery to which he had been called. "Often it was referred to as the 'big folks church.' Revolting against this idea, I was convinced that worship at its best is a social experience with people of all levels of life coming together to realize their oneness and unity under God. Whenever the church consciously or unconsciously caters to one class it loses the spiritual force of the 'whosoever will, let him come' doctrine, and is in danger of becoming little more than a social club with a thin veneer of religiosity."[82]

Some of his sharpest words against the church, however, were to be found in his "Letter from a Birmingham Jail." He complained, "In the midst of blatant injustices inflicted upon the Negro, I have watched white churchmen stand on the sideline and mouth pious irrelevances and sanctimonious trivialities. In the midst of a mighty struggle to rid our nation of racial and economic injustice, I have heard many ministers say, 'Those are social issues, with which the gospel has no real concern.' And I have watched many churches commit themselves to a completely otherworldly religion which makes a strange, un-Biblical distinction between body and soul, between the sacred and the secular."[83]

He wrote about the early Christian martyrs who rejoiced at the opportunity of martyrdom for Christ. In those days the church did not just reflect popular opinion, it transformed the mores of society. But, King felt, things had changed. The contemporary church, he feared, was weak and ineffectual. It tended to defend the status quo. The power structure of the average community took comfort in the church's silent—and often even vocal—sanction of things as they were.

Consequently, King believed that the judgment of God was on the church. If it did not recapture the sacrificial spirit of early Christianity it would lose its authenticity, and people would no longer take it seriously. In fact, King said, "Every day I meet young people whose disappointment with the church has turned into outright disgust."[84]

The true church, for him, was "the inner spiritual church, the church within the church . . . the true *ekklesia* and the hope of the world." Nevertheless, he saw hope in that some courageous leaders in the church had become active in the struggle against segregation. "Some have been dismissed from their churches, have lost the support of their bishops and fellow ministers," he wrote. "But they have acted in the faith that right defeated is stronger than evil triumphant. Their witness has been the spiritual salt that has preserved the true meaning of the gospel in these troubled times."[85] He was also encouraged by the participation of the white churches in the march on Washington in 1963. "Never before had they been so fully, so enthusiastically, so directly involved."[86]

But in *Where Do We Go From Here: Chaos or Community?* he had harsh words for the white church. He saw it as a blatantly racist institution. "The white man ended up making God his partner in the exploitation of the Negro. What greater heresy has religion known?" he asked.[87] Later, in the same book, he said that the white church "has been an accomplice in structuring racism into the architecture of American society. The church, by and large, sanctioned slavery and surrounded it with the halo of moral respectability. It also cast the mantle of its sanctity over the system of segregation."[88]

King insisted that the white church must do two things. First, he said, it has a "duty to lift up its voice like a trumpet and declare unto the people the immorality of segregation. It must affirm that every human life is a reflection of divinity, and that every act of injustice mars and defaces the image of God in man."[89]

But it must do more than just make declarations. The white church, King admonished, "must take the lead in social reform. It must move out into the arena of life and do battle for the sanctity of religious commitments. And it must lead men along the path of true integration, something the law cannot do."[90]

Although he was negative about the white church he was also self-critical toward the black. He described himself as "the son, the grandson, and the great-grandson of preachers." Then he added, "I see the church as the body of Christ. But, oh! How we have blemished and scarred that body through social neglect and through fear of being noncomformists."[91]

In his sermon, "Transformed Nonconformist," he complained about black preachers. "Seduced by the success of symbols of the world, we have measured our achievements by the size of our parsonage. We have become showmen to please the whims and caprices of the people. We preach comforting sermons and avoid saying anything from our pulpit which might disturb the respectable views of the comfortable members of our congregations."[92]

Two types of black churches have failed to be faithful to the gospel, in King's mind. "One," he said, "burns with emotionalism, and the other freezes with classism." The first kind, he said, reduced worship to entertainment, emphasized volume over content and confused spirituality with muscularity." People in such a church, King said, "have more religion in their hands and feet than in their hearts and souls" and have "neither the vitality nor the relevant gospel to feed hungry souls."[93]

The other kind of church, he feared, developed a class system and took pride in its dignity, the professional people in its membership, and its status. The worship service was cold, dull, and uninspiring, and the sermon just a commentary on current events. "The church today," King said, "is challenged to proclaim God's Son, Jesus Christ, to be the hope of all men in all of their complex personal and social problems."[94]

The great triumphant moment in King's career was his speech at the march on Washington on August 28, 1963. He advised those who had suffered in the civil rights movement to have faith in the redemptive power of suffering. He made use of biblical imagery in that speech. "I have a dream that one day every valley shall be exalted, every hill and mountain be made low, the rough places shall be made plain, and the crooked places shall be made straight and the glory of the Lord will be revealed and all flesh shall see it together." In King's faith, this gospel produced freedom. He concluded that speech with the hope that "black men and white men, Jews and Gentiles, Catholics and Protestants will be able to join hands and to sing in the words of the old Negro spiritual, 'Free at last, free at last; thank God Almighty, we are free at last.' "[95]

BIBLIOGRAPHY

Books by Martin Luther King, Jr.:

The Measure of a Man. Philadelphia: The Christian Education Press, 1959.
Strength to Love. New York: Harper and Row, 1963. Paperback edition, Cleveland: William Collins and World, 1963.
Stride Toward Freedom. New York: Harper and Brothers, 1958.
A Testament of Hope: The Essential Writings of Martin Luther King, Jr. Edited by James M. Washington. San Francisco: Harper and Row, 1986.
The Trumpet of Conscience. New York: Harper and Row, 1967.
Where Do We Go From Here: Chaos or Community? New York: Harper and Row, 1967.
Why We Can't Wait. New York: Harper and Row, 1963. Paperback edition, New York: New American Library, 1964.

Books about Martin Luther King, Jr.:

Ansbro, John J., *Martin Luther King, Jr.: The Making of a Mind.* Maryknoll, New York: Orbis Books, 1982.
Bennett, Lerone, Jr., *What Manner of Man: A Biography of Martin Luther King, Jr.* Chicago: Johnson Publishing Company, 1964.
Fisher, William Harvey, *Free at Last: A Bibliography of Martin Luther King, Jr.* Metuchen, NJ: Scarecrow, 1977.

Garrow, David J., *Bewaring the Cross: Martin Luther King, Jr., and the Southern Christian Leadership Conference, 1955–1968.* New York: W. Morrow, 1986.

King, Coretta Scott, *My Life With Martin Luther King, Jr.* New York: Holt, Rinehart and Winston, 1969.

Lewis, David L., *King: A Biography.* Urbana: University of Illinois Press, 1978.

Lincoln, C. Eric, editor, *Martin Luther King, Jr.: A Profile.* New York: Hill and Wang, 1970.

Oates, Stephen B., *Let the Trumpet Sound: The Life of Martin Luther King, Jr.* New York: Harper and Row, 1982. Paperback edition, New York: New American Library, 1985.

Reddick, L.D., *Crusader Without Violence: A Biography of Martin Luther King, Jr.* New York: Harper and Brothers, 1959.

Schulke, Flip and Penelope McPhee, *King Remembered.* New York: Pocket Books, 1986.

Slack, Kenneth, *Martin Luther King.* London: SCM Press, 1970.

Smith, Ervin, *The Ethics of Martin Luther King, Jr.* New York: Edwin Mellen Press, 1981.

Smith, Kenneth L., *Search for the Beloved Community: The Thinking of Martin Luther King, Jr.* Valley Forge, PA: Judson Press, 1974.

Witherspoon, William Roger, *Martin Luther King, Jr.: To the Mountaintop.* Garden City, New York: Doubleday, 1985.

CHAPTER II

Simone Weil

SIMONE WEIL's productive but tormented life was cut short at the age of thirty-four by an uncompromising determination to identify with suffering humanity. She was a social activist of the first rank and a mystic of deep insight. If ever any life combined successfully the virtues of action and contemplation, hers did.

T.S. Eliot described her as a "difficult, violent and complex personality," yet "one who might have become a saint."[1] Andre Gide saw her as "the most spiritual writer of this century." Albert Camus called her "the only great spirit of our time," and George A. Panichas, editor of a collection of her works, insisted that she was "the great Christian Hellenist of modern times, occupying a place commensurate with that of Christian Hellenists like Justin Martyr, Athenagoras, Clement of Alexandria and Origen in the early centuries of the Christian era."[2]

She was born on February 3, 1909 in Paris, the second child of a prosperous physician. The family's apartment overlooked the Luxemburg Gardens. Every material need would be met, but, ironically, Simone chose to live a life of physical deprivation, a choice often frustrated by her parents' generosity.

Although the Weils were Jewish they were agnostic and did not practice the ancestoral faith. Some of the relatives still did, but Simone was not trained in religion in any traditional way. She saw herself as French rather than Jewish, though she would later suffer much because of Nazism. Still, she was always hostile to Judaism and much of the Old Testament, regarding Yahweh as a tyrant who enslaved people.

Her brother André, three years older, was something of a mathematical prodigy and would later in life join the Institute for Advanced Studies at Princeton. Simone was grossly offended by a remark she overheard that André was a genius but she was beautiful. That drove her to suppress her femininity and develop herself intellectually. She learned how to argue brilliantly and dress unattractively. Some people called her "the categorical imperative in skirts."[3]

In 1914 Dr. Weil was called into the French army and the family followed him wherever it was practical. It was at this time that Simone began to exhibit her desire to identify with the reality of human suffering. There are many stories, perhaps legendary, about her early asceticism. She refused to eat sugar as long as the French soldiers were deprived of it and she sent some of her rations to the front. Later she would refuse to wear stockings in the winter in order to be like the street urchins of Paris, although she finally admitted that she did it partly to annoy her affluent parents. Still, the style of her life was going to be to deny herself what the most unfortunate people could not have.

Simone developed into a prodigy herself, although she refused to admit it. At the age of six she was quoting Jean Racine, the French poet. Leslie Fiedler, in his introduction to Weil's *Waiting for God,* reported that at the age of fourteen she went through a spiritual crisis that very nearly ended in suicide. She was overwhelmed by a sense of her complete unworthiness and by almost unbearable migraine headaches. Later she would say that "to know that one is mediocre is 'to be on the true way.' "[4]

In 1919 Weil entered the Lycée Fénelon, a public high school and junior college for girls in Paris and in 1924 began studies in philosophy at the Lycée Victor Duruy. After taking her baccalaureate in philosophy in 1925 she entered the Lycée Henri IV where she was a student of the French philosopher Emile-Auguste Chartier who wrote under the pen name Alain. In 1928 she placed first,

immediately ahead of Simone de Beauvoir, in the entrance examinations to the Ecole Normale Supérieure, where she was one of the
first women to be admitted.

Her intellectual interests were wide-ranging. She studied
Greek, Latin, Sanskrit, modern languages, philosophy, western and
eastern religions, mathematics, science and literature. At an early
age she had been attracted to bolshevism, but at the Ecole Normale
she developed a serious interest in Marxism, pacificism and trade
unionism. In 1931 she attained her *agrégée de philosophie* at age
twenty-two, having written a thesis on *Science and Perception in
Descartes.*

Her first teaching job was at Le Puy. Fiedler described her at
this point in her life as "an earnest and committed radical, though
one who never joined a political party."[5] This was in 1932, in the
depths of the Depression. During school hours she taught philosophy; the rest of the time she participated in demonstrations and
spent time with unemployed workers. Detractors called her "the
Red virgin of the tribe of Levi."[6]

She refused to eat more rations than those on relief and gave
her surplus to the poor. The superintendent for instruction became
disturbed at her radical activity and threatened to withdraw her
license to teach. Weil told him she would consider such an act as
"the crown of her career." He did not follow through on the threat,
but she did transfer to a school at Auxerre for the 1933–34 school
year. Her teaching methods were controversial and the students did
not do well on the exams. The administrator of the school solved
the problem by abolishing the philosophy position on the faculty,
and Weil had no choice but to leave.

Her next teaching post was at Roanne. Here she was known as
a communist and an atheist which, of course, she was not in the
strict sense of those terms. During her years of teaching she participated in miners' marches protesting unemployment and wage re-
ductions, stood with factory workers in strikes and wrote on social
issues for radical publications. She lived on very little and slept only
a few hours at night.

Wanting to experience the lot of the worker, she took a leave
of absence from teaching and worked during the 1934–35 school

year in factories, which she wrote about in the *Révolution Proléta-rienne* under the pen name S. Galois. She lost one job in an electric motor factory because she could not work fast enough. Finally, she went to work in a Renault factory. This adventure ended with an attack of pleurisy. Her parents, refusing to allow her to suffer, took her to Portugal to recover.

Weil left an account of the factory work in her "Factory Journal." She described her frustration with machines which broke down or did not work properly. This always cost her production time, and one of the persistent entries is "didn't make the rate," the production quotas necessary for full pay.

Entry after entry describe her suffering. "The speed is dizzying. Especially when in order to throw yourself into it you have to overcome fatigue, headaches, and the feeling of being fed up." A few days later she entered, "Very violent headache, finished the work while weeping almost uninterruptedly. When I got home, interminable fit of sobbing. No blunders, however, aside from 3 or 4 botched pieces." She reminded herself, "Pleasant warning from the foreman: if you botch them, you'll be fired."[7]

The journal kept meticulous records of the number of pieces produced, the hours worked, and the pay. But the overall impression one receives from this journal is a sense of depersonalization and slavery. For example, "The effect of exhaustion is to make me forget my real reasons for spending time in the factory, and to make it almost impossible for me to overcome the strongest temptation that this life entails: that of not thinking anymore, which is the one and only way of not suffering from it." Her weak constitution, of course, was a major problem. "Only the feeling of brotherhood, and outrage in the face of injustices inflicted on others, remain intact—but how long would all that last. I am almost ready to conclude that the salvation of a worker's soul depends primarily on his physical constitution. I don't see how those who are not physically strong can avoid falling into some form of despair—drunkenness, or vaga-bondage, or crime, or debauchery, or simply (and far more often) brutishness—(and religion?)."[8]

At the end of the journal she concluded, "I came near to being broken. I almost was—my courage, the feeling that I had value as a person were nearly broken during a period I would be humiliated to remember, were it not that strictly speaking I have retained no memory of it. I got up in the mornings with anguish. I went to the factory with dread; I worked like a slave; the noon break was a wrenching experience. Time was an intolerable burden. Dread—outright fear—of what was going to happen next only relaxed its grip on me on Saturday afternoon and Sunday morning." Summing up the whole experience, she said, "The main fact isn't the suffering, but the humiliation."[9]

In a letter to Albertine Thevenon she tried to express what the factory work had meant for her. "It meant that all the external reasons upon which were based my sense of personal dignity, my self-respect, were radically destroyed within two or three weeks by the daily experience of brutal constraint."[10] She noted that she was fully aware of her degradation and worked hard to reestablish her sense of human dignity. She did it by relying on nothing outside of herself.

In her spiritual autobiography she described how factory work had helped her identify with the sufferings of others. "The contact with affliction had killed my youth," she said. "As I worked in the factory, indistinguishable to all eyes, including my own, from the anonymous mass, the affliction of others entered into my flesh and my soul. Nothing separated me from it."[11] She often complained about Marxists who did not experience the life of the workers.

Leaving her parents she went alone into a poor, small Portuguese village on the day of the festival of its patron saint. The visit made an indelible impression on her. She watched the wives of the village fishermen process by the boats, carrying candles and singing what she believed to be "very ancient hymns of a heart-rending sadness." She wrote, "I have never heard anything so poignant unless it were the song of the boatmen on the Volga. There the conviction was suddenly borne in upon me that Christianity is pre-eminently the religion of slaves, that slaves cannot help belonging to it, and I among others."[12]

After her recovery she taught at Bourges for the 1935–36 school year. Again, she gave away most of her salary and continued her radical activities. Although her teaching methods were still unorthodox, this time her students did well on examinations.

In 1936 the Spanish Civil War began and Weil was drawn to it. She joined a unit of anarchists near Saragossa, Spain, and volunteered for several dangerous actions. Her usual physical ineptness betrayed her again when she accidentally spilled boiling oil on her legs. That ended the Spanish adventure, which was fortunate for her since most of the people in her unit were soon killed in action. The injury was severe enough that she had to take a leave of absence from teaching for the next school year, although she continued to write, mostly about peace and labor problems.

As usual, her family came again to an unwanted rescue, taking her on vacations in Switzerland and Italy. In the "Spiritual Autobiography" she reported on "two marvelous days" which she spent at Assisi in 1937. She visited the chapel of Santa Maria degli Angeli where Saint Francis used to pray. There, she said, "something stronger than I was compelled me for the first time in my life to go down on my knees."[13] A latent Christian piety was beginning to emerge.

In the fall of that year she began teaching at St. Quentin but again had to take a sick leave because of her persistent and terribly painful headaches which made her adult life an agony. They went on, she said, even in her sleep.

During the spring of 1938 she spent ten days at the Abbey of Solesmes and attended all the Easter liturgy, captivated by the Gregorian plainsong for which the monastery was famous. It was here that a decisive mystical experience occurred. "I was suffering from splitting headaches," she wrote; "each sound hurt me like a blow: by an extreme effort of concentration I was able to rise above this wretched flesh, to leave it to suffer by itself, heaped up in a corner, and to find a pure and perfect joy in the unimaginable beauty of the chanting and the words. This experience enabled me by analogy to get a better understanding of the possibility of living divine love in the midst of affliction. It goes without saying that in the course of these services the thought of the Passion of Christ entered into my being once and for all."[14]

35

While at Solesmes, Weil met a young English Catholic who introduced her to George Herbert's metaphysical poem "Love." The poem delighted her, she learned it by heart and recited it as a prayer when her headaches were at their worst. It was during the reciting of this poem that she had her first mystical experience. She said that "Christ came down and took possession of me." For the first time she realized the possibility of human contact with the divine. Now, she said, when Christ possessed her "neither my senses nor my imagination had any part; I only felt in the midst of my suffering the presence of love."[15] Her religious feelings would now dominate her thought, although there would be no lessening of social concern.

Her health was still not good enough to resume teaching; in fact, although she did not know it, her teaching career was over.

After the German occupation of Paris the Weil family moved to Marseilles, where her mystical life intensified. In 1940 she was dismissed from the state teaching service under Vichy anti-Jewish laws. In 1941 she met Father J.-M. Perrin and developed a deep friendship in which he became her spiritual director. He sent her to Gustave Thibon, a lay theologian who operated a Catholic agricultural colony in southern France. Thibon resisted the move, believing that intellectuals, especially philosophy graduates, were incapable of prolonged manual work. But Father Perrin's insistence and Thibon's sympathy for persecuted Jews caused him to accept her.

Thibon described her in his introduction to her book *Gravity and Grace.* "She was just then beginning to open with all her soul to Christianity; a limpid mysticism emanated from her; in no other human being have I come across such familiarity with religious mysteries; never have I felt the word *supernatural* to be more charged with reality than when in contact with her."[16] He reported that, although her physical condition was delicate, she worked hard, often eating only blackberries from wayside bushes for her meals. She sent half of her ration coupons to political prisoners each month.

She continued to study philosophy and Sanskrit and tried to lecture to other workers on *The Upanishads.* After several weeks she felt that Thibon was giving her too much consideration and decided to go to another farm where no one knew her so that she might share the lot of real agricultural laborers, following their diets and work schedules. After a month with a team of grape gatherers she rejoined her parents in Marseilles. On May 17, 1942 the family sailed for the United States where it would take an apartment on Riverside Drive in New York.

Weil was unhappy in America. She found the life too secure and could not endure it while the French suffered from Nazism and war. At the same time, she attended daily mass at Corpus Christi Church on 121st Street where Thomas Merton had been baptized.

Returning to France was out of the question, but she was determined to join the resistance. On November 9, 1942 she left her family and sailed for England where she would work for the Free French. Here she produced her book *The Need for Roots,* not actually published until 1949, which included plans for the development of post-war France.

In England she refused to eat more than the rations allowed in France. Weakened by hunger she was forced to enter a hospital where she suffered because of special attention given her. Thibon described the situation: "She had a horror of being given privileges and fiercely shook herself free from any watchful care which aimed at raising her above the common level. She only felt at ease on the lowest rung of the social ladder, lost among the masses of the poor folk and outcasts of this world."[17] On August 17, 1943, she was moved to Grosvenor Sanatorium in Ashford, Kent. Still refusing food, she died on August 24 of starvation and tuberculosis.

Simone Weil had once written, "The death agony is the supreme dark night which is necessary even for the perfect if they are to obtain absolute purity, and for that reason it is better that it should be bitter."[18] After recounting the story of her death Thibon said, "I am a Catholic, Simone Weil was not. I have never doubted for a second that she was infinitely more advanced than I am in the experimental knowledge of supernatural truths, but outwardly she always remained on the borders of the Church and was never baptized."[19]

HUMAN NATURE

Weil believed that human nature was controlled by forces external to individuals, and the only hope for beneficial change was to be found in the grace of God. She described human nature in terms of a spiritual gravity and expressed this in *Gravity and Grace,* a collection of items from her notebooks edited by Gustave Thibon. "All the *natural* movements of the soul are controlled by laws analogous to those of physical gravity," she wrote. "Grace is the only exception. We must always expect things to happen in conformity with the laws of gravity, unless there is a supernatural intervention."[20]

Human relationships, for example, work out on this basis. "What is the reason that as soon as one human being shows he needs another (no matter whether they be slight or great) the latter draws back from him? Gravity."[21]

Gravity draws one down to the lowest levels of living. Weil experienced this in her own life. She admitted, "I must not forget that at certain times when my headaches were raging I had an intense longing to make another human being suffer by hitting him in exactly the same part of his forehead." It is gravity that encourages us to do evil to others. "When in this state I have several times succumbed to the temptation to at least say words which cause pain. Obedience to the force of gravity. The greatest sin."[22]

Gravity and Grace has an aphoristic character about it. One finds statements such as "Creation is composed of the descending movement of gravity, the ascending movement of grace, and the descending movement of the second degree of grace."[23] Human nature causes one to fall, grace causes one to rise, then grace descends. A different kind of movement is described in another aphorism: "To lower oneself is to rise in the domain of moral gravity. Moral gravity makes us fall toward the heights."[24] Weil felt that the more she identified with those at the lower levels of society, the higher she would rise toward God.

People often do evil, she felt, because communicating one's suffering by making others suffer often reduces it. This prompted her to write, "The tendency to spread evil beyond myself: I still

38

have it! Beings and things are not sacred enough to me. May I never sully anything even though I be utterly transformed into mud. To sully nothing, even in thought. Even in my worst moments I would not destroy a Greek statue or a fresco by Giotto. Why anything else then? Why, for example, a moment in the life of a human being who could have been happy for that moment."[25]

Weil believed that one of the major motives in doing evil to another is self-exaltation. "To harm a person is to receive something from him. What? What have we gained when we have done harm? We have gained in importance. We have expanded. We have filled an emptiness in ourselves by creating one in somebody else." Furthermore, she said, "To be able to hurt others with impunity—for instance to pass our anger onto an inferior who is obliged to be silent—is to spare ourselves from an expenditure of energy, an expenditure which the other person will have to make. It is the same in the case of the unlawful satisfaction of any desire. The energy we economize in this way is immediately debased."[26]

It is important, she believed, for people to recognize their limitations. "To grasp that there is a limit and that without supernatural help that limit cannot be passed" she believed was essential. We need to face up to the realities about the world and ourselves. "I am also other than what I imagine myself to be," she wrote. "To know this is forgiveness."[27]

The truth is to be found more in suffering than in pleasure, she believed. "It is human misery and not pleasure which contains the secret of the divine wisdom. All pleasure-seeking is the search for an artificial paradise, an intoxication, an enlargement. But it gives us nothing except the experience that it is vain. Only the contemplation of our limitations and our misery puts us on a higher plane. 'Whosoever humbleth himself shall be exalted.' "

If this is the state of human nature, how can a person possibly love oneself? Her answer was, "God's love for us is not the reason for which we should love him. God's love for us is the reason for us to love ourselves. How could we love ourselves without this motive? It is impossible for man to love himself except this roundabout way."[28]

MYSTICAL EXPERIENCE

Because of her mystical encounters with God, Simone Weil's view of human nature did not drive her to despair.

She did not believe that the mercy of God was evidenced in nature, the created world. She did not elaborate on that point, but her thought emphasized strongly the reality of human suffering which exists in the created world. In fact, she said that Jews, Moslems and Christians are pitiless, yet they talk of divine mercy in nature.

The reason for believing in God's mercy, for Weil, was her mystical experience. In *Gravity and Grace* she wrote, "Those who have had the privilege of mystical contemplation [have] experienced the mercy of God. That is why mysticism is the only source of virtue for humanity. Because when men do not believe that there is infinite mercy behind the curtain of the world, or when they think that this mercy is in front of the curtain, they become cruel."[29]

The best account of Simone Weil's mystical encounters, however, is in her "Spiritual Autobiography," published in *Waiting for God.* It is here that she described how "Christ came down and took possession of me."[30]

She reported that she had never read the writings of the mystics because she never had any need or desire to read them. In fact, she said that God had prevented her from reading them "so that it should be evident to me that I had not invented this absolutely unexpected contact."[31]

Although the experiences in Portugal, Solesmes and Assisi seemed to create within her a receptivity to God, her mystical life steadily deepened around the recitation of the Lord's Prayer. She and a friend, while studying Greek together, decided to learn the Lord's Prayer by heart in the original language. "The infinite sweetness of this Greek text so took hold of me that for several days I could not stop myself from saying it over all the time," she admitted.[32] Gradually she developed the practice of saying it each morning "with absolute attention." If her attention wandered or failed, she would begin all over again until she "succeeded in going through it with absolutely pure attention." She tells us what happened when she did it. "At times the very first words tear my thoughts from my body and transport it to a place outside space where there is neither perspective nor point of view. The infinity of the ordinary expanses of perception is replaced by an infinity to the second or sometimes the third degree. At the same time, filling every part of this infinity, there is a silence, a silence which is not an absence of sound but which is the object of a positive sensation, more positive than that of sound. Noises, if there are any, only reach me after crossing this silence.

"Sometimes, also, during this recitation or at other moments, Christ is present with me in person, but his presence is infinitely more real, more moving, more clear than on that first occasion when he took possession of me."[33]

None of these experiences, however, stopped her personal suffering.

Weil admitted that the problem of God had seemed insoluble to her and that she never really believed that there was any possibility of contact between a person and God. She still found her own mystical experience impossible to believe. "If one could imagine any possibility of error in God, I should think that it had all happened to me by mistake. But perhaps God likes to use castaway objects, waste, rejects," she wrote.[34] Nevertheless, she affirmed in strong terms, "I do not need any hope or any promise in order to believe that God is rich in mercy. I know this wealth of his with the certainty of experience; I have touched it. What I know of it through actual contact is so far beyond my capacity of understanding and gratitude that even the promise of future bliss could add nothing to it for me, since for human intelligence the addition of two infinities is not an addition."[35]

GOD

In her spiritual autobiography Weil wrote that she never sought God at any moment in her life. As an adolescent she saw the God problem "as a problem the data of which could not be obtained here below," and, therefore, she decided to "leave it alone."[36]

"So I left it alone," she said. "I neither affirmed nor denied anything. It seemed to me useless to solve the problem, for I thought that, being in this world, our business was to adopt the best attitude with regard to the problems of this world, and that such an attitude did not depend upon the solution of the problem of God."[37]

The solution to the problem of God for her did not come through intellectual speculation, but through mystical experience. God came to her. This gave her a particular conception of faith. "He who puts his life into his faith in God can lose his faith. But he who puts his life in God himself will never lose it. To put our life into that which we cannot touch in any way. It is impossible. It is death. That is what is required."[38]

Simone Weil sought out and endured suffering in her life because she knew suffering was a major element in human experience and wanted to share in it. Her understanding of God, then, was unusual in that she did not believe that a relationship with God brought an end to suffering. She opposed a popular piety that saw God as the destroyer of human unpleasantness. In *Gravity and Grace* she said, "If we want to have a love which will protect the soul from wounds, we must love something other than God."[39]

She mentioned someone whose family had died under torture, a person who had been the sole survivor of the extermination of a people, and, had she lived longer, she might have mentioned Jews who survived the holocaust. Such people, she believed, would find it impossible to have faith in the mercy of God, or they would understand it in a radically different way. She admitted that she had never been through such experiences, but she knew they existed. Consequently, she said, "I must move toward an abiding conception of divine mercy, a conception which does not change whatever event destiny may send upon me, and which can be communicated to no matter what human being."[40]

In a letter to Father Perrin on her way to America in 1942 she concluded, "The knowledge of this presence of God does not afford consolation; it takes nothing from the fearful bitterness of affliction; nor does it heal the mutilation of the soul. But we know quite certainly that God's love for us is the very substance of this bitterness and this mutilation."[41]

42

In fact, she made the startling statement that if "I were to fall to the bottom of hell, I should nevertheless owe God an infinite debt of gratitude for his infinite mercy, on account of my earthly life, and that notwithstanding the fact that I am such a poor unsatisfactory creature. Even in this hypothesis I should think all the same that I had received all my share of the riches of divine mercy. For already here below we receive the capacity for loving God and for representing him to ourselves with complete certainty as having the substance of real, eternal, perfect and infinite joy. Through our fleshly veils we receive from above presages of eternity which are enough to efface all doubts on this subject."[42]

She found it very difficult to explain the reality of God. In *Gravity and Grace* we find a collection of paradoxical statements. For example, "God exists. God does not. Where is the problem? I am quite sure that there is a God in the sense that I am quite sure my love is not illusory. I am quite sure that there is not a God in the sense that I am quite sure nothing can be anything like what I am able to conceive when I pronounce this word. But that which I cannot conceive is not an illusion." Because God is indescribable and evades conceptualization she wrote, "Of two men who have no experience of God, he who denies him is perhaps nearer to him than the other."[43]

She understood perfectly well why the experience of God is rare. "God could create only by hiding himself," she wrote. "Otherwise there would be nothing but himself."[44] She sensed what all the great mystics have known, that if we experienced the blunt presence of God we would perish. "It is God who in love withdraws from us so that we can love him. If we were exposed to the direct radiance of his love, without the protection of space, of time and of matter, we should be evaporated like water in the sun: there would not be enough 'I' in us to make it possible to surrender the 'I' for love's sake. Necessity is the screen set between God and us so that we can be."[45]

For this reason there must be an element of distance between ourselves and God. Perhaps drawing on the idea of medieval courtly love Weil said, "To love purely is to consent to distance, it is to adore the distance between ourselves and that which we love."[46]

In one fascinating passage in *Gravity and Grace* she warned that we are not to love God as a miser loves his money. If our love is like that we are in for trouble. "It is he who, through the operation of the dark night, withdraws himself in order not to be loved as the treasure is by the miser." In this situation we are tempted to believe that God does not exist, but Weil assured, "If we love God while thinking that he does not exist, he will manifest his existence."[47]

She saw imagination as a hindrance to knowing God. It is impossible to imagine what God is like, yet we face God with all sorts of pre-conceived notions of what the divine is. God must be desired without imagining. "Only desire without an object is empty of imagination. There is the real presence of God in everything which imagination does not veil."[48]

The greatest gift of one's experience with God is joy, for perfect joy exists within God. We can add nothing to it and cannot take anything away from it. Weil said, "Those who wish for their salvation do not truly believe in the reality of the joy within God."[49] What did she mean by this? To want something specific from God is to miss the joy that is always there.

Throughout *Gravity and Grace* Weil stressed the distance between God and humanity and the struggle of the journey to God. "God wears himself out through the infinite thickness of time and space in order to reach the soul and to captivate it. If it allows a pure and utter consent (though brief as a lightning flash) to be torn from it, then God conquers that soul. And when it has become entirely his, he abandons it. He leaves it completely alone, and it has in its turn, but gropingly, to cross the infinite thickness of time and space in search of him whom it loves. It is thus that the soul, starting from the opposite end, makes the same journey that God made toward it. And that is the cross."[50]

The link between God and humanity, for Weil, is love, and love is as great as the distance to be crossed. This love transcends both good and evil, joy and suffering. "Love of God is pure when joy and suffering inspire an equal degree of gratitude," she said.[51]

Love is often a means of attachment to things. Sometimes it is used to attach oneself to an imaginary God. "But to the real God we are not attached," according to Weil, "and that is why there is no cord which can be cut. He enters into us. He alone can enter into us. All other things remain outside, and our knowledge of them is confined to the tensions of varying degree and direction which affect the cord when there is a change of position on their part or on ours."[52]

This is why God is present in everything, good and evil. Weil said that if God can be present through the consecration of a piece of bread in the mass, God can surely be present in extreme evil. The obvious example of this was the cross.[53] Contact with God brings joy whether the contact is in a good or evil situation. Thus, she said, "only the contact matters, not the manner of it."[54]

In a treatise "The Love of God and Affliction" which was published in *Waiting for God* she repeated the theme of God coming to us across the infinity of space and time. She emphasized that the initiative was always with God. "He comes at his own time. We have the power to consent to receive him or to refuse. If we remain deaf, he comes back again and again like a beggar, but also, like a beggar, one day he stops coming. If we consent, God puts a little seed within us and he goes away again. From that moment God has no more to do: neither have we, except to wait. We only have not to regret the consent we gave him the nuptial yes."[55]

The growth of that seed in us proceeds apace, and it may be painful. We have to destroy what gets in its way, both weeds and good grass, hence the real possibility of suffering. Then, she said, "A day comes when the soul belongs to God, when it not only consents to love but when truly and effectively it loves. Then in its turn it must cross the universe to go to God. The soul does not love like a creature with created love. The love within it is divine, increased; for it is the love of God for God that is passing through it. God alone is capable of loving God. We can only consent to give up our own feelings so as to allow free passage in our soul for this love. That is the meaning of denying oneself. We are created for this consent, and for this alone."[56]

In spite of her conception of the distance between God and a person, Weil still had a sense of God at work in the life of the individual. She wrote of "the compulsion of God's pressure" which is exerted on those who deserve it. "God rewards the soul that thinks of him with attention and love and he rewards it by exercising a compulsion upon it strictly and mathematically proportionate to this attention and this love. We have to abandon ourselves to the pressure, to run to the exact spot whither it impels us and not go one step farther, even in the direction of what is good. At the same time we must go on thinking about God with ever increasing love and attentiveness, in this way gaining the favor of being impelled ever further and becoming the object of a pressure that possesses itself of an ever-growing proportion of the whole soul; we have attained the state of perfection."[57]

SUFFERING

There is a sense in which Simone Weil's whole spirit was expressed in a statement in her "Spiritual Autobiography." "Every time I think of the crucifixion of Christ I commit the sin of envy."[58] Affliction is such an integral part of human experience that Weil believed the words of Jesus from the cross, "My God, my God, why hast thou forsaken me," are "the real proof that Christianity is something divine."[59]

Weil believed that God's mercy was felt in affliction as well as in joy—perhaps even more in affliction. Human mercy is almost always revealed when people give joy, but it is different with God's mercy. This does not mean that God makes affliction easy. Affliction is terrible and destructive, she said, and we lie when we deny this. But "If still persevering in our love, we fall to the point where the soul cannot keep back the cry, 'My God, why hast thou forsaken me?', if we remain at this point without ceasing to love, we end by touching something that is not affliction, not joy, something that is the central essence, necessary and pure, something not of the senses, common to joy and sorrow: the very love of God."[60]

In an essay on "The Love of God and Affliction" Weil attempted to define affliction. "It is not the same as simple suffering, like a toothache, that ends with us little worse for the wear. Rather, it takes possession of the soul and marks it through and through with its own particular mark, the mark of slavery." It is "an uprooting of life, a more or less attenuated equivalent of death, made irresistibly present to the soul by the attack or immediate apprehension of physical pain."[61]

It is no surprise that suffering occurs in human life, but Weil was surprised that "God should have given affliction the power to seize the very souls of the innocent and to take possession of them as their sovereign lord. At the very best, he who is branded by affliction will keep only half his soul."[62]

A person suffering affliction will become convinced that God is absent. There seems to be nothing to love, and if one stops loving, God's absence is final. But, she urged, "The soul has to go on loving in the emptiness, or at least to go on wanting to love, though it may only be with an infinitesimal part of itself. Then, one day, God will come to show himself to this soul and to reveal the beauty of the world to it, as is the case of Job. But if the soul stops loving it falls, even in this life, into something almost equivalent to hell."[63]

One of the most devastating things about affliction, for Weil, was the fact that the victim, little by little, becomes its accomplice. This makes it very difficult for a person to work one's way out of affliction, of even wanting deliverance. Even a person who has survived will feel a compulsion to fall back into it. And if a person, through an act of love, helps someone out of the state of affliction, the victim will come to hate the benefactor, so destructive to the soul is affliction.

But, said Weil, God created love and the capacity to love. "He created beings capable of love from all possible distance."[64] The obvious example of distance from God was the crucifixion. "Men struck down by affliction are at the foot of the cross, almost at the greatest possible distance from God."

The tearing apart of God and humanity, which affliction causes, "echoes perpetually across the universe in the midst of the silence, like two notes, separate yet melting into one, like pure and heart-rending harmony. This is the Word of God. The whole creation is nothing but its vibration. Those who persevere in love hear this note from the very lowest depths into which affliction has thrust them. From that moment they can no longer have any doubt."[65]

One of the most frightening aspects in all this is Weil's belief that affliction is arbitrary. It is the result of blind mechanism. The only thing people can do about it is "to keep their eyes turned toward God through all the jolting."[66] If the mechanism were not blind there would be no affliction. Unfortunately, suffering affliction, said Weil, is not a matter of choice, although she herself sought it out many times. However, people who are persecuted for their faith do so out of choice; they could avoid it. This is not affliction. But, she said, "Christ was afflicted. He did not die like a martyr. He died like a common criminal, confused with thieves, only a little more ridiculous. For affliction is ridiculous."[67] When people suffer genuine affliction they share in the experience of the cross when it seems that God is absent.

The mechanism which brings affliction appears from our standpoint to be blind. In fact, however, matter is completely obedient to the will of God. It does what God created it to do. In like manner, one is obedient to God in that one is matter. One may desire obedience or not desire it, but one will be obedient to what God has created. "Each time that we have some pain to go through, we can say to ourselves quite truly that it is the universe, the order and the beauty of the world and the obedience of creation to God that are entering our body. After that how can we fail to bless with tenderest gratitude the Love that sends us this gift."[68]

Weil saw joy and suffering as two gifts which must be fully savored. "Through joy, the beauty of the world penetrates our soul. Through suffering it penetrates our body."[69]

One thing which affliction does, said Weil, is to introduce the soul to "the immensity of force, blind, brutal, and cold." This force, of course, is part of God's creation. Therefore, the person suffering affliction "finds himself nailed to the very center of the universe. It is the true center; it is not in the middle; it is beyond space and time; it is God." The nail pierces all the way through the distance separating God and humanity. "In this marvelous dimension, the soul, without leaving the place and the instant where the body to which it is united is situated, can cross the totality of space and time and come into the very presence of God."[70] That, for Weil, was the positive side of affliction.

In *Gravity and Grace* she wrote a short paragraph adding that affliction itself, however, was not enough. "Unconsoled affliction is necessary. There must be no consolations. No apparent consolation. Ineffable consolation then comes down."[71]

Suffering can have a redemptive benefit if it results in the complete destruction of the "I," the ego. When the "I" has been destroyed "we have there the cross in its fulness. Affliction can no longer destroy the "I," for the "I" no longer exists, having completely disappeared and left the place to God."[72]

Weil's whole outlook on life was based on the idea that suffering and affliction reveal the truth of reality. "How could I ever think an affliction too great," she wrote, "since the wound of an affliction, and the abasement to which those whom it strikes are condemned, opens to them the knowledge of human misery, knowledge which is the door of all wisdom?"[73]

She was attracted to Christianity because all of Christian theology was grounded in the sufferings of the cross. In this sense, a suffering person reveals God. "An innocent being who suffers sheds the light of salvation upon evil. Such a one is the visible image of the innocent God. That is why a God who loves man and a man who loves God have to suffer."[74]

People react to suffering, of course, in different ways. Some go mad, others find God. Weil said, "After having gone through that, some begin to talk to themselves like madmen. Whatever they may do afterward, we must have nothing but pity for them. The others, and they are not numerous, give their whole heart to silence."[75]

THE CHURCH

Simone Weil was never baptized a Christian, but after her mystical experience she regarded herself as a Christian. In a letter which has been called "Hesitations Concerning Baptism" she said,

"I love God, Christ, and the Catholic faith as much as it is possible for so miserably inadequate a creature to love them. I love the saints through their writings and what is told of their lives. . . . I love the six or seven Catholics of genuine spirituality whom chance has led me to meet in the course of my life. I love the Catholic liturgy, hymns, architecture, rites and ceremonies."[76] Later she wrote, "I always adopted the Christian attitude as the only possible one. I might say that I was born, I grew up, and I always remained within the Christian inspiration. While the very name of God had no part in my thoughts, with regard to the problems of this world and this life I shared the Christian conception in an explicit and rigorous manner, with the most specific notions it involves. Some of these notions have been part of my outlook for as far back as I can remember."[77] She even affirmed that "the duty of acceptance in all that concerns the will of God, whatever it might be, was impressed upon my mind as the first and most necessary of all duties."[78]

However, Weil believed that God did not want her in the church. She wrote to her spiritual director, "I have never once had, even for a moment, the feeling that God wants me to be in the Church. I have never even once had a feeling of uncertainty. I think that at the present time we can finally conclude that he does not want me in the Church. Do not have any regrets about it."[79]

She had a deep sense of exile. She simply did not fit in with the world. She said in one letter, "I feel that it is necessary and ordained that I should be alone, a stranger and an exile in relation to every human circle without exception."[80] Only in this way, she felt, could she be her true self.

One of her major problems was the belief that Christianity is catholic by right, but not in fact. It should include all things, but it does not. "So many things are outside it, so many things that I love and do not want to give up, so many things God loves, otherwise they would not be in existence." What did she have in mind? Her list included "all the immense stretches of past centuries except the last twenty are among them; all the countries inhabited by colored races; all secular life in white peoples' countries; in the history of these countries, all the traditions banned as heretical, those of the Manicheans and Albigenses for instance; all those things resulting from the Renaissance, too often degraded but not quite without value." She felt that she would betray the truth if she left that point where she had been since birth, "the intersection of Christianity and everything that is not Christianity."[81]

Weil had a sense of the relatedness of all truth, even religious truth. In her "Spiritual Autobiography" she said that she "came to feel that Plato was a mystic, that all the Iliad is bathed in Christian light, and that Dionysus and Osiris are in a certain sense Christ himself; and my love was thereby redoubled." She wrote of reading the *Bhagavad-Gita* in 1940 which she described as "words with such a Christian sound, put into the mouth of an incarnation of God."[82]

She also had a problem with the church as a social structure. Social institutions have dangerous effects upon people, one of which is to influence them too much. That was what she feared for herself. "My natural disposition," she said, "is to be very easily influenced, too much influenced, and above all by anything collective. I know that if at this moment I had before me a group of twenty young Germans singing Nazi songs in chorus, a part of my soul would instantly become a Nazi. That is a very great weakness, but that is how I am."[83]

While she did not die as a baptized Catholic, surely she took her faith more seriously than most. The combination of social commitment and encounter with Christ produced a remarkable woman whose life exemplified the best in the Christian tradition. In many ways her life was an authentic *imitatio Christi*. No one can boast completely pure motives, but Simone Weil found herself in identification with the poor and suffering of the world, and this brought her into contact with the mercy of God.

BIBLIOGRAPHY

Books by Simone Weil:

Formative Writings 1929–1941. Amherst: University of Massachusetts Press, 1987.

Gateway to God. New York: Crossroad, 1982.

Gravity and Grace. New York: Putnam's, 1952.

Iliad, or, the Poem of Force. Wallingford, Pa.: Pendle Hill, 1956.

Intimations of Christianity Among the Ancient Greeks. London: Routledge and Kegan Paul, 1957.

The Need for Roots. New York: Putnam's, 1952.

The Notebooks of Simone Weil. Two Volumes. London: Routledge and Kegan Paul, 1956.

Oppression and Liberty. Amherst: University of Massachusetts Press, 1973.

Simone Weil, An Anthology. New York: Weidenfeld and Nicolson, 1986.

The Simone Weil Reader. Edited by George A. Panichas. New York: David McKay, 1977.

Waiting for God. New York: Putnam's, 1951.

Books about Simone Weil:

Allen, Diogenes, *Three Outsiders: Pascal, Kierkegaard, Simone Weil.* Cambridge, Massachusetts: Cowley Publications, 1983.

Anderson, David, *Simone Weil.* London: SCM Press, 1971.

Coles, Robert, *Simone Weil: A Modern Pilgrimage.* Reading, Massachusetts: Addison-Wesley, 1987.

Davy, Marie Magdeleine, *The Mysticism of Simone Weil.* London: Rockliff, 1951.

Dunaway, John M., *Simone Weil.* Boston: Twayne Publishers, 1984.

Hellman, John, *Simone Weil: An Introduction to Her Thought.* Philadelphia: Fortress Press, 1982.

Little, J.P., *Simone Weil: A Bibliography.* London: Grant and Cutler, 1973.

McLane-Iles, Betty, *Uprooting and Integration in the Writings of Simone Weil.* New York: Peter Lang, 1987.

Petrement, Simone, *Simone Weil: A Life.* New York: Pantheon, 1976.

Rees, Richard, *Simone Weil: A Sketch for a Portrait.* Carbondale: Southern Illinois University Press, 1966.

Springsted, Eric O., *Christus Mediator: Platonic Mediation in the Thought of Simone Weil.* Chico, Cal.: Scholars Press, 1983.

Springsted, Eric O., *Simone Weil and the Suffering of Love.* Cambridge, Mass.: Cowley Publications, 1986.

Tomlin, Eric Walter Frederick, *Simone Weil.* New Haven: Yale University Press, 1954.

White, George Abbott, ed., *Simone Weil: Interpretations of a Life.* Amherst: University of Massachusetts Press, 1981.

CHAPTER III

Dag Hammarskjöld

DAG HAMMARSKJÖLD's career, culminating in his service as secretary-general of the United Nations, was one of constant success and distinction. Yet with the posthumous appearance of his journal *Markings,* even his closest associates realized that there was a side to this man they had never known, yet which undergirded his whole life and work. Admired for his neutrality and objectivity, Hammarskjöld was also a Christian mystic. Religious feelings motivated his work, but almost no one knew he had such interests. Clifton Anderson, in a review in *The New Republic* for November 24, 1964, said that *Markings* was not what close friends had hoped for as a final testament. "Some consider it with embarrassment, not knowing what to make of so gratuitous an example of discrepancy, unreason and excess, and the more they liked the man the more they wish it had never appeared." In a June 30, 1964 article in *Look,* John Lindberg described *Markings* as "the self-revelation of a man who in the end conceived of himself as a modern avatar, a divine messenger, at the council table on the East River," and raised the question of how it was possible "for this supposedly sober Swede to assume the role of savior on the rostrum of the United Nations without the spectators becoming aware of what was going on."

Henry P. Van Dusen, one-time president of Union Theological Seminary in New York, described Hammarskjöld as "one of the truly great men of this era" and "a Renaissance man at mid-twentieth century."[1] Indeed, his interests were wide-ranging. His field was economics, but he had interests in drama, music, painting, sculpture, mountain climbing, languages, and nature. He loved nothing more than intellectual conversation and regretted it when his friends married and were no longer available for such discussion.

Hammarskjöld was born at Jonkoping, Sweden on July 29, 1905. His father, Hjalmar Hammarskjöld, was a rather unpopular prime minister of Sweden during the World War I years and also served as governor of Uppland. He represented an old conservative Lutheranism and believed strongly that one should do one's duty. Sven Stolpe described him as "a great but detested politician, with considerable resources and brilliant gifts, but with only meager capacity for making direct and warm contact with his fellow men."[2] Dag's mother, on the other hand, had a more evangelical religious outlook and was attracted to the emotional rather than the intellectual. Dag went to church with her regularly, but his friends believed that it was only out of courtesy; someone that brilliant, they believed, had no time for religion.

There were four children in the family, all of whom achieved distinction. The oldest son, Bo, became a provincial governor. Ake eventually became secretary-general of the International Court of Arbitration at The Hague and served as a member of several League of Nations conciliation commissions. The third son, Sten, although troubled by illness most of his life, became a journalist and novelist.

While Hammarskjöld's father was governor of Uppland the family lived in the castle at Uppsala for almost twenty-five years. A major influence on Hammarskjöld during these years was the archiepiscopal palace. He was a childhood playmate with the children of Lutheran archbishop Nathan Söderblom, one of the pioneers of the ecumenical movement who was responsible for a conference on Life and Work held in Stockholm in 1925. This event was one of the milestones leading to the formation of the World Council of Churches. Hammarskjöld attended that conference as an usher. Henry Van Dusen told a story about someone suggesting that the general secretary of the World Council of Churches tell Hammarskjöld something about the ecumenical movement when introduced to him in Geneva. Hammarskjöld replied, "Oh, I know all about that! I was brought up under Söderblom."

Hammarskjöld attended the University of Uppsala where he completed his B.A. in two years. He studied literature, philosophy, French, and economics, but complained to Söderblom's wife, "I thought I should be reading about the progress of ideas through the ages, not wasting attention on the love-affairs of authors."[4]

Gustav Aulén, a Swedish theologian, noted that in Uppsala in the 1920s there was a certain intellectual tension between those with religious and ecclesiastical interests, led by Söderblom, and the so-called "Uppsala school" of philosophy known for its critical attitude toward religion. It is unlikely that Hammarskjöld, with this intellectual interest, would be untouched by such controversy. In *Markings,* Hammarskjöld referred to the struggle between intellectual integrity and faith. He finally resolved the problem by recognizing that the language of faith is different in nature from other kinds of language.

Still, during the 1920s Hammarskjöld kept whatever religious feelings he had to himself. His companions would not have been interested, Stolpe said. "When he tried to touch on deeper themes, on religious and metaphysical aspects of life, they completely failed to understand him."[5] These friends "for the most part were spiritually and religiously unawakened, and to whom he had to speak in another language—a language foreign to his soul."[6]

After completing a doctorate Hammarskjöld entered government service and rose rapidly through the ranks. In 1930 he went to Stockholm with his parents, and for the next ten years there are no entries in *Markings.* He began to work for the Royal Commission on Unemployment, an appropriate agency since his doctoral dissertation at the University of Stockholm was on "The Spread of Boom and Depression." Soon he became under-secretary in the Ministry of Finance and later would concurrently hold the post of chairman of the Bank of Sweden. He developed a reputation for hard work and excessively long hours. In 1946 he renegotiated a trade agreement with the United States and headed a delegation from Sweden that participated in discussions on the Marshall Plan. He became vice-chairman of the Organization for European Economic Cooperation. In 1947 he joined the Ministry of Foreign Affairs in Sweden where he eventually was appointed vice-minister. In 1951 he became vice-chairman of Sweden's UN delegation, ascending to the chairmanship a year later. On April 10, 1953, after the resignation of Norway's Trygve Lie, he was elected to the first of two terms as secretary-general of the United Nations.

Of the many accounts of Hammarskjöld's response to this election, one of the most interesting is that of Bo Besko, an artist who was doing Hammarskjöld's portrait. When Besko suggested to Hammarskjöld that he might be a good man to fill the vacant secretary-general position Hammarskjöld replied, "Nobody is crazy enough to propose me—and I would be crazy to accept." Beskow himself said, "I don't think he felt it a heavy 'duty' to accept—he saw the appointment as a challenge and a chance to do some really useful work. He was pleased and excited."[7]

In 1953, after his election as UN secretary-general, Hammarskjöld was a guest on Edward R. Murrow's radio program. On the air Hammarskjöld presented a statement, a credo, about his life and beliefs. It appeared in print in *The British Weekly,* in *Servant of Peace,* a collection of Hammarskjöld's speeches, and can be found in Van Dusen's *Dag Hammarskjöld: The Statesman and His Faith.*[8]

In the credo Hammarskjöld affirmed that he had inherited from his father's side of the family "a belief that no life was more satisfactory than one of selfless service to your country—or humanity. This service required a sacrifice of all personal interests, but likewise the courage to stand up unflinchingly for your convictions." From scholars and clergymen on his mother's side of the family he inherited "a belief that, in the very radical sense of the Gospels, all men were equals as children of God, and should be met and treated by us as our masters in God." While many of his Swedish friends might have believed that Hammarskjöld shared their agnosticism, this credo is a ringing affirmation of faith. He mentioned the definition of faith used by St. John of the Cross: "Faith is the union of God with the soul." Religious language, he said, is simply a "set of formulas which register a basic spiritual experience." It does not describe sensory reality. Hammarskjöld said that it took him a long time to reach that point in his own thinking, but when he did, the beliefs in which he had been raised "were recognized by me as mine in their own right and by my free choice."

In the remainder of the credo Hammarskjöld revealed the two most important religious influences on him. The first was Albert Schweitzer who taught him that "the ideal of service is supported by and supports the basic attitude to man set forth in the Gospels. In his work I also found a key for modern man to the world of the Gospels."

The Schweitzer influence is an interesting part of Hammarskjöld's religious makeup. Van Dusen reported that on a mountain climb in 1948 Hammarskjöld took along a bulky German volume in which he seemed to be deeply absorbed. It was the original edition of Schweitzer's *The Quest of the Historical Jesus,* and he suggested to his companions that they should read it.

Aulén saw this influence as a rather natural thing. There were many contacts between Schweitzer and Sweden in the 1920s. When his hospital had economic problems, Schweitzer received aid from Söderblom. To raise money he gave Bach organ concerts in Sweden. He also delivered the Olaus Petri Lectures in Uppsala and was obviously well known in Swedish circles. Hammarskjöld had ample opportunity to encounter Schweitzer and be influenced by him.

There appear to be two things which Hammarskjöld received from Schweitzer. The first was a strong emphasis on ethics. In an article he published in a Swedish Social-Democrat journal, *Tiden,* "The Civil Servant and Society," he wrote, "The ethic exemplified by Schweitzer finds expression in the subordination of private interests to the whole: a moral obligation first to the community, in the sense of the nation; secondly to that larger community represented by internationalism."[9] Van Dusen mentioned a letter he received from Schweitzer saying that he had met Hammarskjöld in Switzerland once and that they had similar views on ethics. Schweitzer said that Hammarskjöld was to visit his hospital at Lambarene on the African trip on which he was killed.

Aulen described a second influence from Schweitzer, an emphasis on the humanity of Jesus. Schweitzer's *Quest* struck the field of New Testament scholarship like a thunderbolt. Hammarskjöld seemed impressed with the effort to discover the historical Jesus which presented a picture of him as "a human being, living and acting in a quite distinct historical situation."[10] The reflections on Jesus in *Markings* are not written in christological language, but describe a human being struggling with mission and destiny. This apparently was "the key for modern man to the world of the Gospels" that Hammarskjöld discovered in Schweitzer's writings.

The second major influence on Hammarskjöld which he mentioned in his credo was the medieval mystics. References are made in *Markings* to Meister Eckhart, Thomas a Kempis, and St. John of the Cross. Hammarskjöld had a copy of *The Imitation of Christ* with him on the trip when he died. He said that the lesson learned from these people was "how man should live a life of active social service in full harmony with himself as a member of the community of the spirit." Here is a connection between spirituality and social activism.

The mystics taught him that "self-surrender" was the way to "self-realization." It was "singleness of mind" and "inwardness" that had given them the strength "to say yes to every demand which the needs of their neighbors made them face, and to say yes also to every fate life had in store for them." For them love was "an overflowing of the strength with which they felt themselves filled when living in true self-oblivion. And this love found natural expressions in an unhesitant fulfillment of duty and in an unreserved acceptance of life, whatever it brought them personally of toil, suffering—or happiness."

Finally, Hammarskjöld concluded the credo, "I know that their discoveries about the laws of inner life and of action have not lost their significance."

One other important influence on Hammarskjöld's religious life was, of course, the Bible. *Markings* contains quotations from twenty Old Testament psalms; four of them (4, 60, 62, 73) are quoted twice. There are three quotations from the gospel of John, one from Matthew, one from Revelation, and one each from Genesis and Isaiah. There are several references to the Lord's Prayer. As is the case with most Christian mystics, Hammarskjöld knew the psalter well and often quoted from it at decisive moments in his life. According to Van Dusen's correlation between passages in *Markings* and events in his life, Hammarskjöld entered Psalm 139:8, "If I take the wings of the morning and remain in the uttermost parts of the sea; even there also shall thy hand lead me,"[11] on a journey to Peking to try to negotiate the release of American airmen. In fact, Van Dusen opined that the Bible was far more of an influence on Hammarskjöld than the mystics were after his election to the UN post. At least, there are more references to scripture than the mystics after 1953.

It should not be surprising then, that Jon Söderblom, the son of the bishop, reported that Hammarskjöld once had been "attracted by the idea of studying theology." And Sven Stolpe reports that in 1930, "in the course of many walks together we planned a defence of Christianity, a sort of apologia against the so-called Hagerstrom school of philosophy, which he had studied and thought out but did not fear."[12]

One more aspect of Hammarskjöld's faith must be mentioned, and that was the universality of his religious outlook. He quoted from non-Christian mystics and spiritual writers, "The lovers of God have no religion but God alone."[13] He referred to Chinese, Greek, and Zoroastrian religions. He believed, according to Aulén, that no limits could be placed on God's activity in the world. This universal activity could be recognized in non-Christian religions. Van Dusen said that traditional Christian theology, which Hammarskjöld must have been taught as a child, "appears to have supplied no part of the undergirding of the man's mature faith."[14] Rather, his faith was built upon a sort of practical devotion and his own religious experience.

This interest was seen in one of his most treasured projects at the United Nations, the building of a meditation room. This was to be a place in the UN building where people could find quiet for reflection and stillness. He supervised every detail of the creation of "A Room of Quiet" in 1957. In a leaflet he composed that was to be given to visitors, he said: "People of many faiths will meet there, and for that reason none of the symbols to which we are accustomed in our meditation could be used."[15]

The main symbol of the room was a shaft of light striking a rock, a piece of iron ore. This symbolized, he said, "how the light of the spirit gives light to matter."[16] The stone may appear to be an empty altar. It is empty, said Hammarskjöld, "not because there is no God, not because it is an altar to an unknown god, but because it is dedicated to the God whom man worships under many names and in many forms." There were no other symbols in the room, he said, because he wanted "nothing to distract our attention or to break in on the stillness within ourselves. It is for those who come here to fill the void with what they find in their center of stillness."[17]

Markings is a remarkable book, a diary of thoughts kept throughout Hammarskjöld's adult life, although no entries are precisely dated before 1953. Its existence was unknown until the manuscript was found in his house in New York. Also found was a letter from Hammarskjöld to the Swedish under-secretary for foreign affairs, Leif Belfrage, instructing him to take charge of the diary. Hammarskjöld indicated that he had not originally intended it to be published, but since he had become a public figure, that had changed. Still, he said that he wrote for himself and not for the public. The letter granted permission for publication.

The entries are generally brief, some prose, some poetry. About three-quarters through the book Hammarskjöld explained the purpose of *Markings*. The notes, he said, were "signposts you began to set up after you had reached a point where you needed them."[18] They contained ideas that he believed strongly, but did not want to speak about while he was alive. Now we have them, and they give us rich insights into the life of a remarkable man.

VOCATION

Hammarskjöld had a tremendous sense of vocation, and throughout *Markings* he described his goals. At the beginning of the book he placed a poem:

I am being driven forward
Into an unknown land.

The pass grows steeper,
The air colder and sharper.
A wind from my unknown goal
Stirs the strings
Of expectation.
Still the question:
Shall I ever get there?
There where life resounds,
A clear pure note
In the silence.[19]

Already it is obvious that his goal was not just professional, but had a mystical element about it, a search for a clear pure note in silence. His major vocation was his own self-development. "What you have to attempt—to be yourself." And what kind of self did he hope to be? He prayed that he might become "a mirror in which the greatness of life will be reflected."[20]

Still, Hammarskjöld believed that "we are not permitted to choose the frame of our destiny," but "what we put into it is ours. He who wills adventure will experience it. He who wills sacrifice will be sacrificed." But success, he felt, was not a worthwhile life goal. "Never let success hide its emptiness from you, achievement its nothingness, toil its desolation. And so keep alive the incentive to push on further, that pain in the soul which drives us beyond ourselves."[21] In fact, he wrote later, "I pity the man who falls in love with his image as it is drawn by public opinion during the honeymoon of publicity."[22]

Nevertheless, his hopes for life were joyful and rich. "To exist in the fleet joy of becoming, to be a channel for life as it flashes by in its gaiety and courage, cool water glittering in the sunlight—in a world of sloth, anxiety, and aggression. To exist for the future of others without being suffocated by the present." He praised the person who "has given himself completely to something he finds worth living for."[23]

Throughout *Markings* Hammarskjöld advocated giving oneself to others as a high source of joy. This assumed, however, that one's life had about it something worth giving. In 1951 he wrote, "Excited by the thought of a further sacrifice because life has still not demanded all. Suppose, though, it has already taken all it can use. The wish to give everything is all very fine, provided you have succeeded in so enriching your soul that everything you have to offer is of value. If not—And why so tense? What currents of worldly ambition still course through your striving as a human being?"[24]

There was a strong sense of an awareness of a divine presence in Hammarskjöld's life. He believed that God was working in his life, even though things may not be going as he wished. "When in decisive moments God acts," he wrote, "it is with a stern purposefulness, a Sophoclean irony. When the hour strikes, He takes what is His. What have you to say? Your prayer has been answered, as you know. God has a use for you, even though what He asks doesn't happen to suit you at the moment."[25]

This idea was developed further in a poem in which Hammarskjöld wrote that when one loves life and other people as God loves them, "then He can use you—then, *perhaps,* He will use you." But, Hammarskjöld concluded, "if he doesn't use you—what matter. In His hand, every moment has its meaning, its greatness, its glory, its peace, its co-inherence."[26]

The major key to the success of one's vocation, for Hammarskjöld, was love. No one can accomplish great things without doing little things well. "Without the humility and warmth which you have to develop in your relations to the few with whom you are personally involved, you will never be able to do anything for the many." In fact, he said, "It is better for the health of the soul to make one man good than 'to sacrifice oneself for mankind.' "[27]

Whatever success one has in life must be attributed to God, Hammarskjöld believed. "Rejoice if you feel that what you did was 'necessary,' " he said, "but remember, even so, that you were simply the instrument by means of which He added one tiny grain to the Universe He has created for His own purposes."[28] One must consider whether one works for the glory of God or for one's own glory. "Upon the answer to this question depends the result of your actions."[29]

Hammarskjöld's career was necessarily filled with tension and difficulty, even possible martyrdom. But he rejected completely the idea that God wants us to suffer in order to learn. "How far from this," he said, "is the assent to suffering when it strikes us *because* we have obeyed what we have seen to be God's will."[30] Nevertheless, he saw his own life as a sacrificial act. He wrote a Haiku poem:

> May I be offered
> To that in the offering
> Which will be offered.[31]

OPENNESS TO GOD

During his years in diplomacy Hammarskjöld was not an active churchman, and many people were surprised by the intensity of the religious feelings expressed in *Markings*. The book reveals, however, a strong, almost passionate desire to be open and receptive to God.

In the early pages of *Markings* he raised the question, "How can you expect to keep your powers of hearing when you never want to listen? That God should have time for you, you seem to take as much for granted as that you cannot have time for Him."[32] But listening to God enables one to perceive reality more clearly. "The more faithfully you listen to the voice within you, the better you will hear what is sounding outside."[33] In 1953 he wrote in his journal, "Not I, but God in me."[34] And two pages later we find, "To be, in faith, both humble and proud: That is, to live, to know that in God I am nothing, but that God is in me."[35]

Markings contains many prayers, usually in poetry, such as this one from a 1954 entry:

> Thou who art over us, Thou who art one of us,
>   Thou who *art*—Also within us,
> May all see Thee—in me also,
>   May I prepare the way for Thee,
> May I thank Thee for all that shall fall to my lot,
>   May I also not forget the needs of others,
> Keep me in Thy love
>   As Thou wouldest that all should be kept in mine.

May everything in this my being be directed to Thy glory
    And may I never despair.
For I am under Thy hand,
    And in Thee is all power and goodness.

On the same page he wrote, "The 'unheard-of'—to be in the hands of God. Once again a reminder that this is all that remains for you to live for—and once more the feeling of disappointment which shows how slow you are to learn."[36]

Much is revealed about Hammarskjöld in one of the next entries, "As long as you abide in the Unheard-of, you are beyond and above—to hold fast to this must be the First Commandment in your spiritual discipline."[37]

A person is strongest, Hammarskjöld believed, when the attention is focused on God. "But when his attention is directed beyond and above, how strong he is, with the strength of God who is within him because he is in God. Strong and free, because his self no longer exists."[38] In fact, he felt that the sense of morality in society would be lost completely "had it not constantly been watered by the feeder-stream of power that issues from those who have forgotten themselves in God?"[39]

Hammarskjöld thought much about the relationship between human works in the world and God's providence. It is natural for people to take credit for what God has done. "God sometimes allows us to take the credit for His work. Or withdraws from it into His solitude. He watches our capers on the stage with an ironic smile—so long as we do not tamper with the scales of justice."[40]

But actually the matter is more serious than that. One's life must be lived under God alone. Hammarskjöld noted, "It is not sufficient to place yourself daily under God. What really matters is to be *only* under God: the slightest division of allegiance opens the door to daydreaming, petty conversation, petty boasting, petty malice—all the petty satellites of the death-instinct."[41]

One finds in *Markings* an absence of traditional theological language although there are some biblical quotations, especially from the psalms. The concepts appear to come more from religious mysticism than from orthodox theology. For example, in raising the question of how one is to love God, Hammarskjöld replied, "You must love Him as if He were a non-God, a non-Spirit, a non-Person, a non-Substance: love Him simply as the One, the pure and absolute Unity in which there is no trace of Duality. And into this One, we must let ourselves fall continually from being into non-being. God helps us to do this."[42] No concept is adequate to describe God.

People resist giving their lives to God because they want to be independent, but Hammarskjöld felt that this attitude missed the point. "God desires our independence—which we attain when, ceasing to strive for it ourselves, we 'fall' back into God," he wrote.[43]

Hammarskjöld was certainly orthodox in his doctrine of human nature. He had a sense of original sin, of "that dark counter-center of evil in our nature." Life in God, however, does not allow one to escape from this but is "the way to gain full insight concerning it." It is not this dark side of our character that causes us to create the fiction of religion, he felt. Rather, it is the experience of God that enables us to see ourselves as we really are. "A living relation to God is the necessary precondition for the self-knowledge which enables us to follow a straight path, and so be victorious over ourselves, forgiven by ourselves."[44]

The spirituality of Hammarskjöld is probably best summed up by a statement written in 1957: "The best and most wonderful thing that can happen to you in this life is that you should be silent and let God work and speak."[45]

SILENCE

An important part of Hammarskjöld's spirituality was the high value he placed on silence. There are some things in life, he believed, that needed no words. "Every deed and every relationship is surrounded by an atmosphere of silence," he said. "Friendship needs no words—it is solitude delivered from the anguish of loneliness."[46]

Interior silence is what is most important. "To preserve the silence within—amid all the noise. To remain open and quiet, a moist humus in the fertile darkness where the rain falls and the grain ripens—no matter how many tramp across the parade ground in whirling dust under an arid sky."[47] Similarly, he wrote, "To be able to see, hear, and attend to that within us which *is* there in the darkness and silence."[48]

Finally, he wrote for himself a little litany about stillness:

> Understand—through stillness,
> Act—out of the stillness,
> Conquer—in the stillness.[49]

An entry dated Whitsunday, 1961 explains his own silent religious commitment. "I don't know Who—or what—put the question, I don't know when it was put. I don't even remember answering. But at some moment I did answer *Yes* to Someone—or Something—and from that hour I was certain that existence is meaningful and that, therefore, my life, in self-surrender, had a goal. From that moment I have known what it means 'not to look back,' and 'to take no thought for the morrow.' "[50]

Most of the 1961 entries are poems. The last stanza of one said:

> Thou
> Whom I do not know
> But Whose I am.
> Thou
> Whom I do not comprehend
> But Who hast dedicated me
> To my fate.
> Thou—[51]

MYSTICAL EXPERIENCE

Most people who knew Dag Hammarskjöld were surprised to find that he was obviously a mystic of deep experience. In *Markings* he quoted many Christian mystics, including St. John of the Cross and Meister Eckhart. How did he describe and understand the mystical encounter with God?

Hammarskjöld discussed mystical experience in relation to life in the world. He said that is it "always *here* and *now*—in that freedom which is one with distance, in that stillness which is born of silence. But—this is a freedom in the midst of action, a stillness in the midst of other human beings." However, he did not understand it as an isolated esoteric experience. Rather, he described it as "a constant reality to him who, in this world, is free from self-concern, a reality that grows peaceful and mature before the receptive attention of assent."[52]

There is a strong emphasis on realizing the value of the present moment in *Markings.* "It is *now,* in this very moment, that I can and must pay for all that I have received. The past and its load of debt are balanced against the present. And on the future I have no claim. Is not beauty created at every encounter between man and a life, in which he repays his debt by focusing on the living moment all the power which life has given him as an obligation?"[53]

Life, for Hammarskjöld, had about it the character of an inward journey. Early in *Markings* he mentioned those times of silence when he saw himself as he really was with all of his frailties and weaknesses. The temptation was great to avoid this vision by engaging in much activity. But Hammarskjöld advised, "Gaze steadfastly at the vision until you have plumbed its depths."[54]

In a 1950 entry, Hammarskjöld said, "The longest journey is the journey inwards."[55] One of the terrifying aspects of such an inner look, he believed, was that it often revealed God's presence. "When we are compelled to look ourselves in the face," he wrote, "then He rises above us in terrifying reality, beyond all argument and 'feeling,' stronger than all self-defensive forgetfulness."[56]

There are several entries in the journal which begin with a quotation from the Lord's Prayer, "Thy will be done." One of the things this meant, for Hammarskjöld, was "to let the inner take precedence over the outer, the soul over the world—wherever this may lead you." And then he added a warning not to worry about the value of the spiritual life in the world because sometimes a worldly good will disguise itself as spiritual.[57]

In 1951 he wrote what comes close to being a description of mystical experience. He mentioned overcoming fear of oneself, of others, of the "underlying darkness," and living at "the frontier of the unheard-of." One arrives at the outer limits of knowledge. "But, from a source beyond it, something fills my being with its possibilities. Here desire is purified and made lucid: each action is a preparation for, each choice an assent to the unknown. Prevented by the duties of life on the surface and looking down into the depths, yet all the while being slowly trained and molded by them to take the plunge into the deep whence rises the fragrance of a forest star, bearing the promise of a new affection. At the frontier—"[58]

One of the prerequisites for this development is, according to Hammarskjöld, the ability to love without expectation of any response. "When Love has matured and, through a dissolution of the self into light, become a radiance, then shall the Lover be liberated from dependence upon the Beloved, and the Beloved also be made perfect by being liberated from the Lover."[59]

Then Hammarskjöld raised the question, "In what dimension of time is this feeling eternal? It was, it filled me with its treasurers. Born in me, known to none, it fled from me—yet was created, beyond space and time, from a heart of flesh and blood which shall presently become dust."[60]

In 1952 Hammarskjöld expressed his desire for a mystical encounter. "To break through the barrier which, when I encounter reality, prevents my encountering myself—to break through it, even at the price of having to enter the Kingdom of Death. Nevertheless—what do I long for more ardently than just this? When and how shall I find the occasion to do it? Or is it already too late?" The biggest barrier, he knew, was the fear of what might happen. "Aware of the *consummatio* of the deep sea dive—but afraid, by instinct, experience, education, for 'certain reasons,' of putting my head under water, ignorant, even of how it is done."[61]

Later in 1958 he attempted to describe mystical experience again. "In prayer you descend into yourself to meet the Other, in steadfastness and light of this union, see that all things stand, like yourself, alone before God. And that each of your acts is an act of creation, conscious, because you are a human being with human responsibilities, but governed, nevertheless, by the power beyond human consciousness which has created man. You are liberated from things, but you encounter in them an experience which has the purity and clarity of revelation. In the faith which is 'God's marriage to the soul,' *everything,* therefore, has a meaning." Then he expressed the idea more concisely. "Only when you descend into yourself and encounter the Other, do you then experience goodness as the ultimate reality—united and living—*in* Him and *through* you."[62]

There was a strong natural element in Hammarskjöld's mysticism. In 1950 he wrote an entry that contained certain Taoist overtones. He expressed a desire for "a heart pulsating in harmony with the circulation of sap and the flow of rivers, a body with the rhythms of the earth in its movements."[63] The next year he wrote a similar passage: "As a husband embraces his wife's body in faithful tenderness, so the bare ground and trees are embraced by the still, high, light of the mornings. I feel an ache of longing to share in this embrace, to be united and absorbed. A longing like carnal desire, but directed toward earth, water, sky, and returned by the whispers of the trees, the fragrance of the soil, the caresses of the wind, the embrace of water and light."[64]

Many mystics report that the essence of the mystical experience is a flash of insight. In a 1951 entry Hammarskjöld wrote of a summer March day: "Within the birch tree's slender shadow on the crust of snow, the freezing stillness of the air is crystallized. Then —all of a sudden—the first blackbird's piercing note of call, a reality outside yourself, the real world. All of a sudden—the Earthly Paradise from which we have been excluded by our knowledge."[65]

In another passage written several years later he mentioned "the self-forgetfulness of concentrated attention" in which "the door opens for you into a pure living intimacy, a shared, timeless happiness." In such experiences one becomes aware of what has always been the case but was allowed to be obscured. "Then I saw that the wall had never been there, that the 'unheard-of' is here and this, not something and somewhere else, that the 'offering' is here and now, always and everywhere—'surrendered' *to be* what, in me, God gives of Himself to Himself."[66]

Another traditional characteristic of mystical experience is a sense of the oneness of all things. Hammarskjöld described this also. "In a dream I walked with God through the deep places of creation;

past walls that receded and gates that opened, through hall after hall of silence, darkness, and refreshment—the dwelling place of souls acquainted with light and warmth—until, around me, was an infinity into which we all flowed together and lived anew, like the rings made by raindrops falling upon wide expanses of calm dark waters."[67]

FAITH

Hammarskjöld defined faith in his credo statement on Murrow's radio program as the union of God with the soul. However, he believed that faith could not be rationally comprehended or "true." In fact, it could not be understood without self-knowledge. Only by "pursuing the fleeting light of the depth of our being do we reach the point where we can grasp what faith is."[68]

In the early pages of *Markings* Hammarskjöld revealed his own personal wrestling with faith. He was held back, he said, by "an intellectual hesitation which demands proofs and logical demonstration." But, he confessed, "Through me there flashes this vision of a timeless magnetic field in the soul, created in a timeless present by unknown multitudes, living in holy obedience, whose words and actions are a timeless prayer."[69]

One aspect of faith, Hammarskjöld said, is to be both humble and proud, "to live, to know that in God I am nothing, but that God is in me."[70] However, he concluded that faith simply is; "it cannot be comprehended, far less identified with the formulae in which we paraphrase what is."[71]

Hammarskjöld rejected the idea that miracles can be the ground of faith. "We act in faith—and miracles occur," he wrote, but miracles do not prove faith. If people need miracles they lose confidence in faith on its own. "Faith *is,* faith creates, faith carries. It is not derived from, nor created, nor carried by anything except its own reality."[72] Furthermore, faith does not necessarily cause triumphs. He saw humiliation as "the necessary precondition and consequence of faith." The crucifixion would not have the same meaning for us if Jesus had been "crowned with the halo of mar-

71

tyrdom."[73] To understand Christ that event must be seen as a humiliation.

CHRISTIANITY

Christian faith is not something one searches out, Hammarskjöld felt, but rather it is something that seeks the individual. That is why he remained faithful to it. But his Christianity was not a self-serving kind of religion that is supposed to provide all sorts of benefits. Rather it exacted a high price from its followers. In 1953 Hammarskjöld wrote, "He who has surrendered himself to it knows that the Way ends on the Cross—even when it is leading him through the jubilation of Gennesaret or the triumphal entry into Jerusalem."[74] There are dangers in becoming a serious Christian. It may lead to loneliness. It even requires physical self-denial, and if one fails, the body will claim back what it was denied "in forms which it will no longer be in your power to select."[75]

Elsewhere in the book he wrote, "I came to a time and place where I realized that the Way leads to a triumph which is a catastrophe, and to a catastrophe which is a triumph, that the price for committing one's life would be reproach, and that the only elevation possible to man lies in the depths of humiliation. After that, the word 'courage' lost its meaning, since nothing could be taken from me."[76]

The key to understanding Christianity, for Hammarskjöld, was Christ himself. In his Whitsunday, 1961 entry he wrote, "As I continued along the Way, I learned, step by step, word by word, that behind every saying in the Gospels stands one man and one man's experience. Also behind the prayer that the cup might pass from him and his promise to drink it. Also behind each of the words from the Cross."[77]

There are many entries in which Christ is the object, or in which Hammarskjöld obviously had in mind a Christ figure. For example, early in the book he wrote of one who "bore failure without self-pity, and success without self-admiration. Provided he knew he had paid his uttermost farthing, what did it matter to him how others judged the result?"[78]

One of the finest passages in *Markings* is a 1951 entry, rather lengthy in comparison with the others, in which he described Christ as "a young man, adamant in his committed life." He washed his disciples' feet knowing "that no one of them had the slightest conception why he had to act in the way that he must. He knew how frightened and shaken they would all be." Christ was the Son of God in that he was "absolutely faithful to a divine possibility," and walked "the road of possibility to the end without self-pity or demand for sympathy, fulfilling the destiny he [had] chosen—even sacrificing affection and fellowship when the others are unready to follow him—into a new fellowship."[79]

Much later in the book Hammarskjöld discussed Jesus' associations with publicans and harlots. He did not do that to gain their support or to convert them by appeasement. He did it, Hammarskjöld said, because his humanity was "rich and deep enough to make contact even in them, with that in human nature which is common to all men, indestructible, and upon which the future has to be built."[80] And near the end of the book there is a poem in which Christ says,

> Soon, now, the torches, the kiss:
> Soon the gray of dawn
> In the Judgment Hall.
> What will their love help there?
> There, the question is only
> If I love them.[81]

HUMAN NATURE

Any serious social activist must have worked out in his or her own mind an understanding of human nature, what humanity is and whether it and its institutions can be changed. Hammarskjöld knew that humanity is exceedingly complex. He wrote a Haiku poem:

> This accidental
> Meeting of possibilities
> Calls itself I.[82]

He also knew that even modern psychology cannot understand fully the mystery of our humanity. "How easy Psychology has made it for us to dismiss the perplexing mystery with a label which assigns it a place in the list of common aberrations."[83]

Hammarskjöld found it difficult to understand humanity, but he had an idea about what it was supposed to be. "To be free and responsible. For this alone was man created."[84] But this freedom has its problems. "The responsibility for our mistakes is ours, but not the credit for our achievements. Man's freedom is a freedom to betray God. God may love us—yes—but our response is voluntary."[85]

People must make choices about themselves, and the choices are many. "Body and soul contain a thousand possibilities out of which you can build many I's. But in only one of them is there a congruence of the elector and the elected. Only one which you will never find until you have excluded all those superficial and fleeting possibilities of being and doing with which you toy, out of curiosity or wonder or greed, and which hinder you from casting anchor in the experience of the mystery of life, and the consciousness of the talent entrusted to you which is your *I*."[86] And in another poem he warned,

> It is with yourself
> That you must live.[87]

Hammarskjöld believed that we lose our freedom to the extent that we are alienated from God. "The intense blaze of your anxiety reveals to what a great extent you are still fettered, still alienated from the One. However, don't worry about this or anything else, but follow the Way of which you are aware, even when you have departed from it. 'Nevertheless, not as I will, but as Thou wilt.' "[88] Elsewhere, he concluded "God desires our independence—which we attain when, ceasing to strive for it ourselves, we 'fall' back into God."[89]

This alienation from God expressed itself in many ways. In one meditation Hammarskjöld wrote, "Looking down through the jade-green water, you see monsters of the deep playing on the reef."[90] These monsters, he felt, were the monsters of self-interest, a constant in the human condition. He asked for the grace that "our self-interest, which is inescapable, shall never cripple our sense of humor."[91] There was a certain interior disgust in the man, expressed when he wrote, "It is not the repeated mistakes, the long succession of petty betrayals—though, God knows, they would give cause enough for anxiety and self-contempt—but the huge elementary mistake, the betrayal of that within me which is greater than I—in a complacent adjustment to alien demands."[92]

One of the obvious manifestations of original sin, which he described as "that dark counter-center of evil in our nature," was the tendency "which rejoices when disaster befalls the very cause we are trying to serve, or misfortune overtakes even those whom we love." Giving ourselves to God does not destroy this, but helps us recognize its presence in us. Only the experience of "religious reality," he said, forces this dark side of our nature into the light. "It is when we stand in the righteous all-seeing light of love that we can dare to look at, admit, and consciously suffer under this something in us which wills disaster, misfortune, defeat to everything outside the sphere of our narrowest self-interest." A deep relationship with God is "the necessary precondition for the self-knowledge which enables us to follow a straight path, and so be victorious over ourselves, forgiven by ourselves."[93]

But Hammarskjöld saw sin even in areas others would not take too seriously. For example, it was present in efforts to be sociable, to say something trivial only so not to be silent, "to rub against one another in order to create the illusion of intimacy and contact." These are examples of "*la condition humaine*" which exhaust us "like any improper use of our spiritual resources."[94]

The whole book is a record of introspection. Hammarskjöld believed that the only thing that could save people was "fully conscious self-scrutiny."[95] But he also warned against an obsession with the evil within. Such self-scrutiny must serve a useful purpose. "Not to brood over my pettiness with masochistic self-disgust," he wrote, "not to take a pride in admitting it—but to recognize it as a threat to my integrity of action, the moment I let it out of my sight."[96] The recognition of this inner reality provided the biggest challenge. "Are you satisfied because you have curbed and canalized the worst in you?" he asked. This is clearly not enough. "In any human situation, it is cheating not to *be,* at every moment, one's best. How much more so in a position where others have faith in you."[97]

One of the biggest problems any human being faces is the problem of ego, and Hammarskjöld recognized that in himself. "Reason," he said, "tells me that I am bound to seek my own good, seek to gratify my desires, win power for myself and admiration from others." But in the perspective of history, when one thinks of the millions of years the world has existed and the countless human lives that have lived through the centuries, the individual becomes insignificant. "Nothing could be less important," he knew, than his own ego. The only thing that really mattered was "a vision in which God *is.*"[98]

The ego can become such a source of trouble. "It was when Lucifer first congratulated himself upon his angelic behavior that he became the tool of evil."[99] And Hammarskjöld wrote of himself, "So, once again, you chose for yourself—and opened the door to chaos. The chaos you become whenever God's hand does not rest upon your head." But when one is "in God," one is "strong and free, because his self no longer exists."[100] The same thought was expressed in a poem from 1959:

> I ask: what am I doing here?
> And, at once, this I
> Becomes unreal.[101]

So, the task becomes one of getting rid of the ego. "Your life is without foundation," Hammarskjöld insisted, "if in any matter, you choose on your own behalf."[102] One of the things that inflates the ego is a refusal to commit oneself to others. "Your ego love doesn't bloom unless it is sheltered. The rules are simple: don't commit yourself to anyone, and therefore, don't allow anyone to come close to you. Simple—and fateful. Its efforts to shelter its love created a ring of cold around the Ego which slowly eats its way inwards towards the core."[103]

To become an authentic person, one must let go. "To let go the image which, in the eyes of this world, bears your name, the image fashioned in your consciousness by social ambition and sheer force of will. To let go and fall, fall—in trust and blind devotion. Towards another, another. . . . To reach perfection, we must all pass, one by one, through the death of self-effacement. And, on this side of it, he will never find the way to anyone who has passed through it."[104]

Finally, Hammarskjöld defined maturity as "a new lack of self-consciousness—the kind you can only attain when you have become so entirely indifferent to yourself through an absolute assent to your fate. He who has placed himself in God's hand stands free vis-à-vis men: he is entirely at ease with them, because he has granted them the right to judge."[105]

In spite of all the negative things Hammarskjöld said about human nature, he had a strong sense of the harmony between all natural elements. He felt that people should not just observe "the interplay of its thousand components," but should "each find a way to chime in as one note in the organic whole."[106] There is even a harmony between people, he believed. "Keeping in step with the measure under the fixed stars of the task. How many personal failures are due to a lack of faith in this harmony between human beings, at once strict and gentle."[107]

While original sin may be a reality in everyone, Hammarskjöld had a positive, hopeful view of human possibilities. In a passage expressing arrogance toward another he confessed, "There is nobody from whom you cannot learn. Before God, who speaks through all men, you are always in the bottom class of nursery school."[108] He wrote a beautiful passage about the good person. "The aura of victory that surrounds a man of good will, the sweetness of soul which emanates from him—a flavor of cranberries and cloudberries, a touch of frost and fiery skies."[109]

TEMPTATION AND ASCETICISM

Even for the most faithful religious person, temptation is an ever present reality. Most temptations have to do with the ego. A troubled spirit, said Hammarskjöld, is often caused by seeking honor for oneself. When one gives in to this one can no longer transform a weakness into a strength. "So you were 'led into temptation,' " he wrote, "and lost that certainty of faith which makes saying Yes to fate a self-evident necessity, for such certainty presupposes that it is not grounded in any sort of a lie."[110]

Every virtue has its own temptations. Those virtues by which one would do the will of God can also be used "for other purposes than His glory. The more He demands of us, the more dangerous are the raw materials he has given us for our achievement. Thank Him then—His gift is also the keys to the Gates of Hell."[111]

Hammarskjöld quoted Titus 1:15, "To the pure all things are pure," but he added, "If a man can only reach this state by making compromises, then his striving is itself an impurity. In such matters there are no differences of degree."[112]

The real power of temptation is felt only by those who have known God, Hammarskjöld believed. "He who has once been under God's hand, has lost his innocence: only he feels the full explosive force of destruction which is released by a moment's surrender to temptation."[113]

It is the ever present reality of temptation that makes some kind of asceticism necessary for the religious person. The dark forces within must be tamed in some way; if allowed to flourish they will destroy a person. In an early entry Hammarskjöld wrote, "You cannot play with the animal in you without becoming wholly animal, play with falsehood without forfeiting your right to truth, play with cruelty without losing your sensitivity of mind. He who wants to keep his garden tidy doesn't reserve a plot for weeds."[114]

There are times when one accepts certain principles and ideas in one's life, but when they become realities the sacrifices required appear to be too great. In 1957 Hammarskjöld wrote a revealing little passage about himself. "You told yourself you would accept the decision of fate. But you lost your nerve when you discovered

78

what this would require of you: then you realized how attached you still were to the world which has made you what you were, but which you would now have to leave behind. It felt like an amputation, a 'little death,' and you even listened to those voices which insinuated that you were deceiving yourself out of ambition. You will have to give up everything. When, then, weep at this little death? Take it to you—quickly—with a smile die this death, and become free to go further—one with your task, whole in your duty of the moment."[115]

GIVING TO OTHERS

If one were to sum up Hammarskjöld's philosophy of life, it would be that the most meaning and the most good are to be found in giving oneself to others. In 1953 he wrote, "Goodness is something so simple: always to live for others, never to seek one's own advantage."[116] Later, in 1958, recognizing that he had only a few more years of life, he said, "The only value of a life is its content—for others. Apart from any value it may have for others, my life is worse than death. Therefore, in my great loneliness, serve others."[117]

Hammarskjöld believed that his life would be judged on the basis of his capacity to love. But being open to others in love is not always an easy thing to do. Early in the book he set down these two lines: "The Strait Road—to live for others in order to save one's soul. The Broad—to live for others in order to save one's self-esteem."[118] But he raised the question, "Is my contact with others anything more than a contact with reflections? Am I not too 'sensible and well balanced,' that is to say, 'too self-centered socially to surrender to anything less than a necessity?"[119] And, he pondered, may one "exist for the future of others without being suffocated by their present?"[120] He chided himself, "Do you really have 'feelings' any longer for anybody or anything except yourself—or even that? Without the strength of a personal commitment, your experience of others is at most aesthetic."[121]

He recognized, however, that living for others does not mean personal annihilation. "Don't be afraid of yourself," he said; "live your individuality to the full—but for the good of others. Don't copy others in order to buy fellowship, or make convention your law instead of living the righteousness."[122] Sometimes, he knew, our reaching out to others fails because "we have never dared to give ourselves. Yet today, even such a maimed experience brought you into touch with a portion of spiritual reality which revealed your utter poverty."[123]

But the rewards are great, for only in giving ourselves to other people can we seek reality as it actually is. In the normal sense such living does not give us anything, necessarily. "But," Hammarskjöld recognized, "in its world of loneliness it leads us up to summits with wide vistas—of insight."[124]

SOCIAL RESPONSIBILITY

Hammarskjöld had a strong sense of personal responsibility to society. Without love life has no meaning. "Life will judge me by the measure of the love I myself am capable of, and with patience according to the measure of my honesty in attempting to meet its demands, and with an equality before which the feeble explanations and excuses of self-importance carry no weight whatsoever."[125]

Although Hammarskjöld was obviously a mystic, he was not guilty of a narcissistic ignorance of the needs of the world. "In our era," he wrote, "the road to holiness necessarily passes through the world of action."[126]

But he was well aware of the complexities of conscientious social action. No revolutionary, he believed, can ignore the society that produced him or her. "To separate himself from the society of which he was born a member will lead the revolutionary, not to life but to death, unless, in his very revolt, he is driven by a love of what, seemingly, must be rejected, and therefore, at the profoundest level, remains faithful to that society."[127]

A career in politics made Hammarskjöld painfully aware of what is involved in "the art of the possible." There is in *Markings* an anguished passage: "The most dangerous of all moral dilemmas:

when we are obliged to conceal truth in order to help the truth to be victorious. If this should at any time become our duty in the role assigned us by fate, how strait must be our path at all times if we are not to perish."[128]

While he personally had many great commitments in his life, Hammarskjöld believed that the true value of a person's work is found on a different level. "The 'great' commitment all too easily obscures the 'little' one. But without the humility and warmth which you have to develop in your relations to the few with whom you are personally involved, you will never be able to do anything for the many. Without them, you will live in a world of abstractions, where your solipsism, your greed for power, and your death wish lack the one opponent which is stronger than they—love."[129]

DEATH

Throughout the pages of *Markings* Hammarskjöld seems to have been preoccupied with the question of death. Did he anticipate the nature of his own death?

One of his earliest entries was:

> Tomorrow we shall meet,
> Death and I—
> And he shall thrust his sword
> Into one who is wide awake.
> But in the meantime how grievous the memory
> Of hours frittered away.[130]

Later he wrote the same thought in different words. "When days and years are fused into a single moment, its every aspect illumined by the light of death, measurable only by the measure of death."[131]

Some passages seem to indicate death is an escape. Hammarskjöld wrote much about loneliness. "Loneliness is not the sickness unto death," he wrote. "No, but can it be cured except by death? and does it not become harder to bear the closer one comes to death?"[132] But he also had positive thoughts about loneliness and death. "Pray that your loneliness may spur you into finding something to live for, great enough to die for."[133]

In a very early passage he argued that the acceptance of death makes many other things in life bearable, or perhaps even insignificant. "There is only one path out of the steamy dense jungle where the battle is fought over glory and power and advantage—one escape from the snares and obstacles you yourself have set up. And that is—to accept death."[134]

But by 1957 he had concluded, "Do not seek death. Death will find you. But seek the road which makes death a fulfillment."[135]

In one particularly moving passage Hammarskjöld described the patient suffering of a neighbor. "I observe her, behind the window across the street, playing patience, day after day, evening after evening. Patience, patience! Probably death will not keep you waiting much longer now."[136]

Death, Hammarskjöld said, does not bring an end to one's life. The effects and influences of what one has done live on. "The consequences of our lives and actions can no more be erased than they can be identified and duly labeled—to our honor and our shame. "The poor ye have always with you.' The dead, too."[137]

Hammarskjöld's anticipation of death was strong and usually positive. In one passage he seemed to think that an authentic encounter with himself would only come with death. "Birth and death, love and pain—the reality behind the dance under the daylight lamps of social responsibility. To break through the barrier which, when I encounter reality, prevents my encountering myself —to break through it, even at the price of having to enter the Kingdom of Death. Nevertheless—what do I long for more ardently than just this? When and how shall I find the occasion to do it. Or is it already too late?"[138]

And in 1951 he wrote, "This evening I would say Yes to the execution squad, not out of exhaustion or defiance, but with an untroubled faith in the co-inherence of all things—to sustain this faith in my life among men."[139]

Hammarskjöld's anticipation of death is remarkable. One should prepare for it well, he said. "Your body must become familiar with its death—in all its possible forms and degrees—as a self-evident, imminent, and emotionally neutral step on the way towards the goal you have found worthy of your life."[140]

In 1951 he wrote, "If even dying is to be made a social function, then, please, grant me the favor of sneaking out on tiptoe without disturbing the party."[141] Four years later he seemed to sense that the reality of death was coming closer. "In the old days," he said, "Death was always one of the party. Now he sits next to me at the dinner table: I will have to make friends with him."[142]

His feelings were perhaps best summed up in his statement, "The hardest thing of all—to die, *rightly.*—An exam nobody is spared—and how many pass it? And you? You pray for strength to meet the test—but also for leniency on the part of the Examiner."[143]

Many commentators have suggested that Dag Hammarskjöld had a premonition of his own death. The last years of his life had been particularly difficult. Attacks on him by the communists were fierce. A civil war in what is now Zaire occupied much of his attention, and in September of 1961 he had flown to Africa in the hope of mediating a peace. He spent his last night with the head of the UN mission to the Congo and left in that house a German copy of Martin Buber's *I and Thou* and his personal copy of *The Imitation of Christ.* Hammarskjöld was using as a bookmark in *The Imitation* a card on which was typed his oath of office.

The next day, around midnight, the DC-6 on which he was flying to Ndola, Northern Rhodesia, to meet Moise Tshombe, president of secessionist Katanga Province, crashed under mysterious circumstances. The only survivor, a UN security guard, said that he heard explosions just before the crash. Speculation has centered on possible sabotage or an attack by a fighter plane. It could have been only an accident. Whatever happened, the world lost a great statesman whose work was undergirded by a deep spirituality.

BIBLIOGRAPHY

Books by Dag Hammarskjöld:

Markings. New York: Knopf, 1964.
Servant of Peace: Speeches by Dag Hammarskjöld. New York: Harper and Row, 1962.

Books about Dag Hammarskjöld:

Aulén, Gustaf, *Dag Hammarskjöld's White Book.* Philadelphia: Fortress Press, 1969.
Beskow, Bo, *Dag Hammarskjöld: Strictly Personal.* Garden City, NY: Doubleday, 1969.
Kelen, Emery, *Hammarskjöld.* New York: Putnam's, 1966.
Lash, Joseph P., *Dag Hammarskjöld: Custodian of the Brushfire Peace.* Garden City, NY: Doubleday, 1961.
Simon, Charlie May, *Dag Hammarskjöld.* New York: Dutton, 1967.
Stolpe, Sven, *Dag Hammarskjöld: A Spiritual Portrait.* New York: Scribner's, 1966.
Thorpe, Deryck, *Hammarskjöld: Man of Peace.* Ilfracombe: Stockwell, 1969.
Urquhart, Brian, *Hammarskjöld.* New York: Knopf, 1972.
Van Dusen, Henry Pitney, *Dag Hammarskjöld: The Statesman and His Faith.* New York: Harper and Row, 1964.

CHAPTER IV

Dorothy Day

DOROTHY DAY was truly one of the saints of the twentieth century. She did not like that designation. "That's the way people try to dismiss you," she told someone in 1977.[1] She devoted her life to the poor and to victims of injustice, always living on the edge of absolute poverty. Cesar Chavez said, "She was for us a kind of beacon, a lighthouse, showing the way of faith in an unclear, turbulent world. She was always there, always visible, always true to her deep spirituality, always true to the poor."[2] Daniel Berrigan described her as "a phenomenal presence whose greatness and goodness had descended full blown in our midst. She seemed always to have been what she was: serene, graced with her aura of piety and pity."[3] She founded a movement that manifested itself in a newspaper, in "houses of hospitality" in the midst of the poor, and, most of all, in her personal presence. She was a classic example of one whose life produced a marriage of spirituality and social action.

Who was this remarkable woman who made such an impact on people, and what led her from a bohemian life of Greenwich Village radicalism to devout Catholicism and service to the poor?

Dorothy Day was born in Brooklyn on November 8, 1897, the third of five children, daughter of a sportswriter who specialized in horse racing. The family moved to Berkeley, California when Dorothy was six, and later on to Oakland. The San Francisco earthquake made a deep impression on her and was one of her earliest encounters with the human suffering that would later dominate her life. After that catastrophe, the Day family went to Chicago and lived in near poverty as her father tried to write fiction. He was a remote man, and Dorothy Day's mother was the unifying force in the family. Although Mr. Day had an interest in the Bible, the family never went to church, and the children were not baptized. As a child Day did attend the Episcopal Church by herself and was impressed by the liturgy. She was also strongly influenced by seeing the Catholic mother of one of her friends at prayer and would call this her first impulse toward Catholicism.

It is not surprising that Day would one day become a journalist. She grew up influenced by the journalism of her father, and three of her brothers would later enter the same profession. However, Mr. Day felt that it was no vocation for a woman and discouraged his daughter from considering that field.

She developed a social conscience early in life. In high school she read widely on her own and was influenced by Dostoevsky, Tolstoy and Kropotkin. She became interested in American radicalism and loved the novels of Jack London and Upton Sinclair. These books surely contributed to her developing sensitivity to the poor.

She received a Hearst scholarship to attend the University of Illinois, where she developed her characteristically independent spirit. Attending class only when she felt like it, she worked at several jobs and sometimes went without food in order to buy books. She joined the Socialist Workers' Party and abandoned whatever religious orientation she might have had after a professor said in a class that strong people did not need religion. She felt a deep kinship with the masses, the poor, and wondered why so much energy was spent reforming society rather than preventing social evils in the first place.

During her sophomore year her family moved to New York, and she began to feel homesick. She rejoined them and tried to find work as a journalist, but her father told the editors in town not to hire her. She eventually went to work for *The Call,* a socialist paper, where she covered strikes, workers' protests and the peace movement. She interviewed Leon Trotsky and had contact with radical women leaders such as Emma Goldman and Elizabeth Gurley Flynn.

When America entered World War I in 1917, Day left *The*

Call and went to Washington to protest the draft. Upon her return to New York she became a writer for *Masses,* described by Nancy L. Roberts as "the most exciting little radical magazine of the day."[4] It was edited by Max Eastman, and its writers included John Reed and Floyd Dell, whose assistant Day would be. Her associations would be with leftist intellectuals, and her life was built around all-night discussions in local taverns.

Six months after Day joined *Masses* the government supressed it under the 1917 Espionage Act. She was not indicted since her byline did not appear on the offending articles, but the magazine did shut down. Unemployed again, Day went to Washington once more, this time to picket the White House for women's suffrage. The result of this was a thirty-day jail sentence which was one of the major trials of her life.

A moving account of this experience was recorded in her auto-biography, *The Long Loneliness.* Day's sentence was for thirty days, and the women who had been arrested immediately began a hunger strike. She described the first six days of her stay in prison as six thousand years. "I lost all consciousness of any cause," she wrote. "I had no sense of being a radical, making protest against a government, carrying on a nonviolent revolution. I could only feel darkness and desolation all around me." The experience would have a major influence on her later life. "I would never be free again," she said, "never free when I knew that behind bars all over the world there were women and men, young girls and boys, suffering constraint, punishment, isolation and hardship for crimes of which all of us were guilty."[5]

The second day she was in prison she asked for a Bible, and received it on the fourth day. She had mixed feelings about the Bible, however. While it brought back some pleasant childhood memories, she was still resisting serious religion. "I clung to the words of comfort in the Bible, and as long as the light held out, I read and pondered. Yet all the while I read, my pride was fighting on. I did not want to go to God in defeat and sorrow. I did not want to depend on Him. I was like the child that wants to walk by itself. I kept brushing away the hand that held me up. I prayed and did not know what I prayed."[6]

When she returned to New York she joined the staff of *Liberator,* the successor to *Masses,* edited by Max Eastman. She was now established as part of the Greenwich Village literary and social avant-garde and began to develop a friendship with Eugene O'Neill, the young playwright. It was also at this time that she began to drop in at St. Joseph's Church on Sixth Avenue for early morning mass after an all night session in a bar. She described her feelings in *The Long Loneliness:* "Many a morning after sitting all night in taverns or coming from balls at Webster Hall, I went to an early morning Mass at St. Joseph's Church on Sixth Avenue and knelt in the back of the church, not knowing what was going on at the altar, but warmed and comforted by the lights and silence, the kneeling people and the atmosphere of worship."[7]

Her Greenwich Village friends now included John Dos Passos, Malcolm and Peggy Baird Cowley, Caroline Gordon, Allen Tate, Kenneth Burke and Hart Crane. They were liberal, radical and bohemian. Many of them remained friends and some would stop by the Catholic Worker house to see her years later. Her leftist colleagues accused her of being too religious to be a good radical or communist. At this point of her life she was influenced by the New Testament, Kempis, *The Imitation of Christ* and Dostoevsky.[8] She thought much about her involvement in social causes and did become attracted to nonviolence as a means of social change, a conviction that she would keep the rest of her life and would occasionally cause her serious trouble.

Finding her life lacking purpose, she took up nurse's training at a hospital in Brooklyn, but gave it up after a year, deciding that journalism was her true calling. The next few years of her life were melancholy. She had an affair with a newsman, Lionel Moise, which resulted in an abortion. Soon after that she married Barkeley Tobey and went to Europe. The couple separated after only a brief time, and Day moved to Chicago where she held a variety of jobs including modeling for artists and working as a sales clerk.

It was in Chicago that she had another jail experience. While visiting a suicidal friend at an IWW rooming house, the place was raided by police and both women charged with prostitution. After she had spent several days in prison the charges were dropped, but the humiliation was severe. The suffering of the other prisoners impressed her deeply. In her autobiography Day commented, "I think that for a long time one is stunned by such experiences. They seem to be quickly forgotten, but they leave a scar that is never removed."[9]

The next stop in Day's journey was New Orleans where she wrote for the New Orleans *Item*. It was while here, in 1924, that she had her novel *The Eleventh Virgin* published. She received $2,500 for the movie rights which allowed her to return to New York and buy a small house on the beach on Staten Island. She renewed her ties with her former radical and literary friends and entered into a common law marriage with Forster Batterham. She wrote for *New Masses* and experienced a brief period of happiness. However, her spiritual interests began to develop once more, much to the unhappiness of Batterham. When she became pregnant, he became more distant. The birth of a daughter, Tamar Teresa, however, was a source of incomparable joy for Day, and she was motivated to have the child baptized. She knew that to do so would mean the end of her relationship with Batterham, and the decision was painful.

The baby was baptized in July 1927; Day herself was baptized in December and became a Catholic. She felt that the Catholic Church was the church of the poor. She was not naive about its problems but she said, "My very experience as a radical, my whole make-up, led me to want to associate myself with others, with the masses, in loving and praising God. Without even looking into the claims of the Catholic Church, I was willing to admit that for me she was the one true Church."[10]

She held a number of jobs after the break-up with Batterham, including one as a scriptwriter in Hollywood. It was a dismal experience. She went to Mexico City and wrote articles about the poor there for *Commonweal*. Near the end of 1932, in the depths of the Depression, she went to Washington to cover the hunger march for *Commonweal*. She was frustrated by the lack of Catholic leadership in dealing with the social problems caused by unemployment. On December 8 she went to the Shrine of the Immaculate Conception in Washington and prayed that some way would be found for her to work for the poor. Her prayer was soon answered when she returned to her apartment in New York and found Peter Maurin waiting for her.

Peter Maurin was a French peasant who had entered the Christian Brothers order, but later joined Le Sillon, a French progressive Catholic group that was interested in political and social issues. Finally becoming disillusioned with the group he worked at various odd jobs while developing intellectually. He was greatly influenced by the anarchist Peter Kropotkin and by French philosophers Léon Bloy, Charles Péguy and Jacques Maritain, as well as the British Catholic writers Hilaire Belloc and G.K. Chesteron.

Eventually Maurin went to Canada and worked as a laborer. In 1925 he moved to New York where he seems to have had a major religious experience. He adopted a life of voluntary poverty, working just long enough to keep body and soul alive. He loved to read at the New York Public Library and he spent much time around Union Square talking with whoever might listen to him. During a hospital stay he listed his occupation as "agitator." He developed a philosophy of radicalism based on Christian action, but he needed someone who had the talent to present his ideas to the world. An editor of *Commonweal* suggested that he contact Dorothy Day. When he finally met her in her apartment, a tremendous and fateful confrontation took place.

Maurin took it as a personal mission to develop Day's Catholic intellectual background. He gave her some of the spiritual classics to read and instructed her in church history and the lives of the saints. His major effort was devoted to convincing her that his analysis of the social order could produce action. It was he who persuaded Day, a professional journalist, that she should begin a newspaper to promote social action based on Catholic teaching. The result was the founding of the *Catholic Worker.* In her excellent study of the history of the *Catholic Worker,* Nancy L. Roberts described the reasons for the success of the paper. "Together, Day and Maurin succeeded where neither alone likely could have. Maurin became the movement's theoretician while Day, always practical, carried out his plan with a few of her own variations. Without Dorothy Day, Peter Maurin probably would have spent the rest of his life lecturing unceasingly to unhearing audiences in Union Square. And without Peter Maurin, Dorothy Day perhaps would have never discovered the life's work that would compel her for the next forty-eight years."[11]

In the winter of 1933 Dorothy Day began planning the first issue of the *Catholic Worker.* Her purpose was to develop a paper that would promote "radical social action based on Christian principles."[12] The time was the worst months of the Depression and the first issue, which appeared on May 1, 1933, carried articles on unemployment, trade unions, cooperatives, the exploitation of blacks, child labor and a local strike. Peter Maurin objected. He had wanted a paper that would be a philosophical journal based heavily on his own essays. He did not see social reform based on strikes or other kinds of mass action; he wanted to promote a radical Christian personalism. The *Worker* did include many of his "Easy Essays," as Day called them, and includes them today.

The *Catholic Worker* was an example of advocacy journalism. Maurin believed that the paper should not just report the news, but the right comment must be given on the news. It was not enough, he said, to report that a man died and left an estate of two million dollars. It must also be said that he left so much money behind because he did not know how to give to the poor for Christ's sake. Day stated in the paper, "We are quite frankly propagandists for Catholic Action."[13] Still, the paper has resisted political partisanship over the years. Day and Maurin never saw politics as a means of social reform.

The *Catholic Worker* was, and still is, the world's best journalistic bargain. Its standard price has been a penny a copy, but often it is simply given away. Ideally, it was to appear monthly; sometimes its financial dependence upon contributions dictated combining issues. By the end of 1987 it was publishing eight times a year.

For its first issue 2,500 copies were printed to be sold in Union Square. By November of that year the number had increased to 20,000. Circulation reached a peak of 190,000 in 1938. The number declined during World War II because of the paper's (and

Day's) absolute pacifist stand. By 1984 circulation had stabilized around 104,000.

The Catholic Worker was the name of a newspaper; it was also the name of a movement which, among other things, established houses of hospitality where a person without resources could find food and shelter. A purpose statement, often published in the paper, said that "The general aim of the Catholic Worker Movement is to realize in the individual and in society the expressed and implied teachings of Christ." The principles of the movement called for a rejection of capitalism as far as that is possible and the establishment of a "distributist" economy. This would be a decentralized economy, one in which workers would own the means of production and distribution. The use of cooperatives and the elimination of an employer class would be accomplished by revolution from below rather than a political revolution which comes from above. Such a revolution must be pacifist. "Otherwise, it will proceed by force and use means that are evil and which will never be outgrown, so that they will determine the *end* of the revolution and that end will again be tyranny."[14]

Peter Maurin felt that the Catholic Worker program should be based on three kinds of activity: (1) Round-table discussions for clarification of thought; (2) houses of hospitality where "works of mercy," corporal and spiritual, could be practiced and taught; (3) farming communes which would lead to decentralization of a capitalistic economy.[15]

All of these things were attempted. The first house of hospitality was Day's apartment. So many people came that another location was secured. That lasted a year, and a house on Mott Street was donated to the Catholic Workers. Here they remained for fifteen years. At the end of 1987 St. Joseph House was located at 36 East First Street in New York. There is also a Mary House for women at 55 East Third. These houses provide sleeping accommodations and meals for the homeless. In 1939 Sheed and Ward published Day's book, *House of Hospitality,* which described in vivid detail the life in a Catholic Worker house: fights among residents, the filth of the poor and drunk and addicted, the hopelessness of the human condition for many, and those obscure acts of mercy that bring hope and relief. Later, Catholic Worker houses were founded in other cities in America. News of them often appears in the *Catholic Worker.*

Peter Maurin's desire for round-table discussions for the clarification of thought was also fulfilled. Scheduled sessions at the Catholic Worker house were often lively, so much so that little clarification actually took place. Well-known Catholic speakers were often present on such occasions. These events continue today in the form of Friday night meetings, advertised regularly in the *Catholic Worker.* Announced topics include Thomas Merton, liberation theology, militarization, and nonviolence.

There were also efforts made at setting up farming communes. The prevailing anarchistic philosophy, however, hindered their success. No one was really in charge, and inevitable quarreling among the residents often led to failure. One of these, Peter Maurin's farm on Staten Island, was a favorite retreat for Dorothy Day.

The most visible part of the movement to most people, however, was the newspaper, the *Catholic Worker.* Dorothy Day described it by saying: "We are not just a newspaper. We are a revolution, a movement. We are propagandists of the faith. We are the Church. We are members of the Mystical Body. We must all try to function healthily. We do not have the same function, but we all have a vocation, a calling. Ours is a 'prophetic' one."[16]

In the July-August 1962 issue of the *Catholic Worker* Day told of being asked by a cardinal in Montreal about the position of the newspaper in the church. She replied that she was one of a group of Catholics writing about "the great problems of the day" which she listed as "the role of the State in man's life, war and peace, means and ends." They were under no bishop and were "free to explore all possibilities of reform and restoration without committing the hierarchy to dangerous positions, and to try to rebuild the social order to make a better society 'where it is easier for men to be good.' "[17] And in 1963, while discussing a trip to Rome, she wrote, "I came away from Rome more convinced than ever that the particular vocation of the *Catholic Worker* is to reach the man in the street, to write about the glorious truths of Christianity, the great adventures of the spirit, which can effect so great a transformation in the lives of men if they would consent to the promptings of the Spirit."[18]

SPIRITUALITY

There are many things to be learned about Dorothy Day in the pages of the *Catholic Worker,* but one thing that came through clearly was her own spirituality. One of the best sources for studying that was her regular column. It was first called "Day After Day," later "Day by Day," and, finally, "On Pilgrimage" as it has been known since 1946.

Dorothy Day had very definite feelings about the style of people in her movement. She was a committed pacifist and believed that nonviolence was the only way to achieve the ends of the Catholic Worker. She also believed in the virtues of poverty, chastity and obedience. The larger virtue, however, was community. "What we really are," she said, "and try to be in all the Catholic Worker Houses around the country, is a family—and gentleness and loving kindness is the prevailing mood."[19]

Not everyone agreed with the Catholic Worker approach. In 1969 she noted that people in the peace movement felt that the Worker effort of taking care of the poor was like applying a band-aid to cancer. But for Day it was important to care for the wounded while trying to slay the giant. What kept the Worker movement going, at least for Day, was the twenty-fifth chapter of the gospel of Matthew. "We are commanded over and over again by Jesus Christ Himself to do these things. What we do for the least of these, we do for Him. We are judged by this."[20]

One of the most frequently quoted statements of Dorothy Day was a summary of the aims and purposes of the Worker movement that appeared in 1940 and many times thereafter. "What we do is very little. But it is like the little boy with a few loaves and fishes. Christ took that little and increased it. He will do the rest. What we do is so little we may seem to be constantly failing. But so did He fail. He met with apparent failure on the Cross. But unless the seed fall into the earth and die, there is no harvest. Our work is to sow. Another generation will reap."[21]

She appreciated the problems of the young. The Catholic Worker accomplished so little that she could understand why they might question nonviolence.[22] Even members of the Worker movement were tempted to despair. The Catholic Worker houses of hospitality were basically flophouses and souplines. "Can't we ever get beyond this? Is this all we can do?" Day often asked. The love which Christ commands was, for Day, a harsh and dreadful thing. "It is hard to see the dear sweet Christ in many a pestering drunk that comes in demanding attention," she said. But her faith was that "these staggering, unlovely, filthy ones who come in waving a bottle at you and cursing you . . . are God's messengers."[23]

There were two specifically religious elements that Day believed were essential to the movement. First, she said, "We must practice the presence of God." This meant that Worker leaders and as many others as possible should go to mass every day. They must receive "food for the soul." She was convinced that "as our perceptions are quickened, and as we pray that our faith be increased, we will see Christ in each other, and we will not lose faith in those around us, no matter how stumbling their progress is." She felt that it was easier to believe that God would supply their material needs than to see Christ in other people.[24]

Second, the work of indoctrination would keep the movement from losing its vision. By indoctrination she meant "giving a reason for the faith that is in us." An essential belief of the Catholic Worker was the fatherhood of God. This idea, Dorothy said, "involves the racial question, it involves cooperatives, credit unions, crafts; it involves Houses of Hospitality and Farming Communes. It is with all these means that we can live as though we believed, indeed, that we are all members of one another."[25]

Dorothy Day often wrote about her own religious experience. While she was not raised as a religious child and moved in intellectual circles that might have been hostile to faith, she was eventually drawn to Christianity and, specifically, Roman Catholicism. But it did not come easily to her. In one of her columns she wrote about her religious feelings in a jail cell after she had been arrested in a demonstration. She said that she felt a sense of shame about turning to God. "I thought there was something ignoble about calling for help in my despair, at my first taste of real destitution, of utter helplessness in the face of the vast sufferings of the world. I read the Scriptures. It was the only book we were allowed in jail. But I was ashamed and turned away in the pride of youth for another dozen years."[26]

There was a strong sensual element in Day's spirituality, and she was drawn to faith through several media. She was particularly moved by sense impressions received in church: "Music speaking to the ear, the incense to the sense of smell, the appeal of color to the eye, stained glass, ikons and statues, bread and wine to the taste, the touch of rich vestments and altar linens, the touch of holy water, oils, the sign of the cross, the beating of the breast."[27] Natural beauty also played a part. She spoke of a time "when the material world around me began to speak in my heart of the love of God."[28]

The Bible was important. She spoke frequently of reading the psalms and often quoted from other books. She had a sense of the presence of God in scripture. "It thrilled me to think of it—God everywhere so palpably present—truly there, if not in the Sacrament of the Altar then in the Book. All should have the Bible in their homes!"[29] Late in her life, in 1977, she wrote an appeal in her monthly column in the *Catholic Worker,* "I need a Bible, large print. I read so much, my eyes tire."[30]

One of the most important sources of revelation for Day, however, was other people. She did not see faith as something easy. "Lord, I believe, because I want to believe," she wrote and said that faith, much like love, is an act of will or preference. But, she affirmed, "God speaks. He answers these cries in the darkness as He always did." The primary revelation of God's presence for Day, however, was the poor, and this was the basic motivation for her commitment to hospitality. "He is incarnate today in the poor, in the bread we break together. We know Him and each other in the breaking of bread."[31]

The notion of Christ present in other people was spelled out more fully in an article Day wrote called "Room for Christ." It was written for the Christmas issue of the *Catholic Worker* in 1945 and reprinted in the December 1980 issue. She expressed her faith that Christ is always with people, but he speaks through the voice of others. It is "with the eyes of store clerks, factory workers and children that He gazes: with the hands of office workers, slum dwellers and suburban housewives that He gives. It is with the feet of soldiers and tramps that He walks, and with the heart of anyone in need that He longs for shelter. And, giving shelter or food to anyone who asks for it, or needs it, is giving it to Christ."[32]

This was not an easy sensitivity to develop. She once told of riding home from a meeting in Brooklyn on a bus, facing a few poor people. "One of them," she wrote, "a downcast, ragged man, suddenly epitomized for me the desolation, the hopelessness of the destitute, and I began to weep. I had been struck by one of those 'beams of love,' wounded by it in a most particular way. It was my own condition that I was weeping about—my own hardness of heart, my own sinfulness. I recognized this as a moment of truth."[33]

These were the people for whom Christ commanded that hospitality be given. Day felt that when she offered food and shelter to those in need she was functioning as Lazarus or Martha or Mary and that the guest was Christ. No halos appeared, but that is not the way Christ is present. She mentioned that Mary did not appear as described in the book of Revelation as a woman clothed in the sun with twelve stars on her head and the moon under her feet. Such an appearance would have impressed people, but Day knew "that wasn't God's way for her nor is it Christ's way for Himself now, when He is disguised under every type of humanity that treads the earth."[34]

So, when people give help or hospitality to another person, they are doing so to Christ. "What a simplification of life it would be," she wrote, "if we forced ourselves to see that everywhere we go is Christ, wearing out socks we have to darn, eating the food we have to cook, laughing with us, walking with us, silent with us, sleeping with us."[35]

PRAYER

There can be no doubt that Dorothy Day's basic motivation for the humanitarian work she did was fundamentally religious. She once mentioned an experience she had in jail trying to convince another inmate that "what she wanted was God, that what we all wanted was God, a sense of well-being, the beatific vision. That vision was described as the marriage feast, as union with the bridegroom in the Bible. Nothing else was going to satisfy us."[36]

This was not just interior piety; it was basic to social reform. For Day, the Catholic Worker goal was "to make that kind of society where it is easier for men to be good . . . and counter the hopelessness of ever achieving that kind of society in our lifetime by hearty prayer."[37]

Day believed that prayers are always answered no matter how impossible the situation. "Even in the midst of horror, one suddenly feels the touch of God's hand and knows . . . that somehow or other 'all will be well.' "[38]

Prayer was a dominant theme in many of her columns. In 1973 Day said, "I must write about prayer because it is as necessary to life as breathing. It is food and drink." She believed that "it brings health to the soul, which needs exercise just as the body does."[39] Referring to some ideas of Gregory the Great, she noted that "If we put ourselves too fervently in Church or State affairs, or let ourselves be too upset, we are weakening, or even nullifying our most potent weapons—the weapons of the spirit."[40]

Dorothy Day was interested in various ways of praying. She had, of course, been a journalist, and writing was a natural activity for her. "Writing, keeping a journal, can be a way of praying," she said.[41]

She was also interested in praying the psalms. The Office of Compline was prayed every evening in the Catholic Worker house. She would occasionally recommend various breviaries or prayer books for her readers to use in their own lives. She often mentioned the use at the Catholic Worker house of the *Short Breviary* which was published by the Liturgical Press in Collegeville, Minnesota.

While she encouraged corporate prayer at the Catholic Worker, she had a strong personal commitment to praying the psalms. "In these days of almost hysterical fear of war and annihilation it is good to read the psalms morning and evening." When one does this "one is praying with the Church and obtaining that confidence in God and His care of us that makes for a peaceful heart."[42] She was encouraged by the growth of prayer groups among Catholics. This development, she said, "does not mean a slackening of the struggle for peace and justice, but a strengthening of it."[43]

Her personal prayer discipline consisted of praying the psalms morning and evening and the Our Father three times a day on her knees. She did mention that there were verses in the psalms that she ignored because they did not speak to her. For example, she did not like the line, "A thousand shall fall at thy side, and then ten thousand at thy right hand, but it shall not come nigh to thee," from Psalm 91. Day's response was, "I prefer the words, 'God wills that all men be saved.' I don't want to see my fellow men falling all around me."[44] She also mentioned from time to time books on the psalms that interested her. The most frequently noted was C.S. Lewis' *Reflections on the Psalms.* She also mentioned a little psalm book arranged for daily reading by a Father Frey. She told a story of an incident involving that book which delighted her. While traveling to the West Coast on a train for a speaking engagement she awoke early in the morning and saw the Pullman porter sitting in an empty compartment reading Father Frey's book.[45]

She was also interested in the Jesus Prayer ("Lord Jesus Christ, Son of God, have mercy on me, a sinner") of the Eastern Orthodox tradition which is popularly described in the Russian spiritual classic *The Way of a Pilgrim.* She found it particularly helpful in stressful situations. "Sometimes the house is like the reception ward at Bellevue Psychiatric [Hospital]. One can only bow one's head to the storm and pray. The Jesus Prayer helps me."[46] In one of her columns she expressed her dismay over the occupation and holding of hostages at the B'nai B'rith and Moslem headquarters in Washington and the assassination of a Chilean exile. The violence in the land overwhelmed her and she wrote, "Recalling the little Russian classic, *The Way of a Pilgrim,* I resolved to begin again an attempt to 'pray without ceasing.' "[47]

Near the end of the 1960s Dorothy Day became aware of a growing Catholic charismatic movement. She attended a number of charismatic prayer meetings and was greatly impressed. In a 1969 column she described a meeting in Michigan. "In Ann Arbor I went to a Pentecostal meeting at the Newman Center. I have never heard more beautiful singing. Prayer ran like a murmur through the hall, and I thought of the breath of the Spirit passing over the waters. There was one speaking with tongues, brief and clear, though I do not know what language it could have been, and there was an interpretation. There was a scattering of older people in the group of worshippers, but mostly they were all young. The mood of waiting, of expectancy, was strong. Here was faith."[48]

She saw this kind of activity as a preparation for battle with the forces of evil. Referring to the Vietnam war, she wrote, "All those at that meeting were going out to a hostile world, a world of such horrors just this last week that it is hard to see how happiness can ever come to us again. I accuse the government itself, and all of us, because we are Americans, too, of these mass murders, this destruction of villages, this wiping out of peoples, the kidnapping, torture, rape and killing that have been disclosed to us so vividly this past month. But meanwhile in this hushed room there was prayer, for strength to know and love and to find out what to do and set our hands to useful work that will contribute to peace, not to war."[49]

She found the charismatics supportive of her work. Some had given blankets and other things to the Catholic Worker. But she wished for a deeper and more radical social concern. "I only wish that the cause of peace, the rejection of war and service in the armed forces, and refusal to pay income tax could be a part of their way of life."[50]

Naturally, Day was appreciative of the communitarianism of the charismatic movement. She was mindful of the many charismatic communities that had been established in the United States. "No longer will families fight a solitary struggle to survive," she noted.[51]

She also appreciated their interest in the renewal of scripture reading and told of a Worker house member: "Rosemary Morse was up early, reading Scripture, but brought me food for the body and a hot cup of coffee. Then she worked all afternoon, mending the screen door, and on the roof, stopping leaks. The Pentecostal movement had made her an avid reader of Scripture. She is a living example of co-ordination—the active, the contemplative, and the ecumenical life. But the roof still leaks."[52]

THE MASS

The Roman mass was central in the faith and experience of Dorothy Day. In a 1962 column she stated that it was the joy of the birth of her daughter that brought her to faith, and that joy had been renewed daily through the mass. When she first became a Catholic she feared that regular mass attendance would be monotonous, but she found it not to be so. The mass, she said, "is an act, a sacrifice, attended by prayers, and these prayers repeated daily, of adoration, contrition, thanksgiving, supplication are always there. One or another emotion may predominate but the act performed evokes the feeling of 'performing the work of our salvation.' "[53]

The mass, she felt, "which is the heart of our life, brings us into the closest of all contacts with our Lord Jesus Christ, enabling us literally to 'put on Christ' and to begin to say "Now, not I live, but Jesus Christ in me.' "[54]

In fact, Day said that it was regular attendance at mass that led to the founding of the Catholic Worker. As she received communion every day she prayed, "Lord, what would you have me to do? Lord, here I am." Then she met Peter Maurin, and the movement began.[55] And it was the mass that has caused her to persevere in the movement. "I would not dare write or speak or try to follow the vocation God has given me to work for the poor and for peace, if I did not have this constant reassurance of the Mass, the confidence the Mass gives."[56]

So the mass became a source of renewal in the midst of the miseries she daily faced. She wrote in her 1962 fall appeal for funds, "I have just returned to Chrystie Street and St. Joseph's House, and if it were not for daily Communion at Mass, bringing confidence and strength, one could not bear the communion with human destitution and the fears which lead to madness in these times of crisis which was so concentrated around us."[57]

Day did have some serious criticism of the mass. For example, she complained that "most priests rush through the Mass as though they were going to forget the words unless they say them as fast as possible. Not only the Latin which is garbled so that it sounds like magic, but also the vernacular." She added, "I am begging them not to. I am begging them to speak as if the words were holy and inspired with power in themselves to produce in us the understanding—the participation that should change our lives."[58]

She was also concerned about too much informality in conducting the mass. "I am afraid I am a traditionalist," she said, "in that I do not like to see Mass offered with a large coffee cup as a chalice. I suppose I am romantic too, since I loved the Arthur legend as a child and reverenced the Holy Grail and the search for it."[59] She was also traditional in her understanding of the mass, that when the words of Jesus, "This is my body," and "This is my blood," were recited by the priest, the bread and wine changed into the true body and blood of Christ.[60] However, she was upset about so many churches being locked so things would not be stolen. Priests worried about the desecration of the Blessed Sacrament. Day thought that was absurd, "as though the dear Lord could not take care of Himself."[61]

She was especially unhappy about offering mass for the military on Hiroshima Day. "Today we are celebrating—how strange, to use such a word—a Mass for the military, the 'armed forces.' No one in charge of the Eucharistic Congress [which she was attending] had remembered what August 6th means in the minds of all who are dedicated to the work of peace." She added, "I plead, in this short paper, that we will regard that military Mass, and all our Masses today, as an act of penance, begging God to forgive us."[62]

POVERTY

Life at the Catholic Worker was a life of poverty. "We admit we are beggars and we are not ashamed of it. We will work as hard as we can, with no salary and trust in the Lord to care for those He sends us." Day then used an image that expressed her whole philosophy of life: "So we remain in the cities, the gutter sweepers of the diocese, working yet beggars, destitute yet possessing all things; happy because today the sun shines, there is a symphony on the radio, children are playing in the streets and a church around the corner where we receive our daily bread."[63]

Dorothy Day was committed to poverty both as a Christian virtue and as a source of freedom and joy. "We need to get to that state of mind where we reject prosperity and embrace poverty, to find the freedom St. Francis sang about."[64] It was a difficult ideal to achieve, she knew, and she felt she had to keep talking about it to remind people of the possibilities. She mentioned that many of the college students she talked with on her trips had never considered voluntary poverty as a means toward peace. She insisted that there was a difference between voluntary poverty and destitution. Voluntary poverty could be a source of beauty and joy.

But there was a practical dimension to poverty in the field of religious work. Religion, Day believed, was open to justifiable criticism if it neglected the needs of the poor and promised an afterlife of prosperity. However, "if those professing religion shared the life of the poor and worked to better their lot and risked their lives as revolutionaries do," then the promise of future glory might have more substance.[65] The work of the Catholic Worker, said Day, "is founded on voluntary poverty and the works of mercy, the latter practiced with the means provided by poverty, our own acceptance of a life without visible means of support."[66] However, a year later, in 1966, while writing about the difficulties of finding a new building for the Worker house, she admitted, "In these inflationary times it is no longer possible to live as we did at the beginning of the Catholic Worker. To try to be poor in an affluent society is hard indeed."[67]

MORALITY

Dorothy Day had strong moral convictions. Some might have called her puritanical. In one of her "On Pilgrimage" columns in the *Catholic Worker* she complained of the lack of what she thought was basic morality on the part of some of those involved in the civil rights movement. Specifically, she was concerned about the dangers of illicit sex and alcohol.

She wrote frequently about sex in the 196Js. "I can only write what I truly believe," she said, "and that is that outside of marriage, and to some extent inside of marriage, there must be a fine regard for chastity and purity, and emphasis on their necessity." She saw sex as a great gift, "a mighty force in man, his creative power." She had lived with Forster Batterham for many years and had given birth to a child out of wedlock, a child she dearly loved. She had known an active sex life. But now she saw a great virtue in making a sacrifice, in giving up sex. "When marriages are broken up by death and separations the unwilling celibate has the power to offer this great gift to God—no trivial gift this sex, so often used in life as a plaything." She concluded with a "plea for penance, a giving up of so great, beautiful, powerful and even terrible thing . . . an offering worthy of God. . . . It is seeing sex in its context, marriage in its perspective. It is a plea for penance. It is a plea for purity of all the senses, through voluntary mortification."[68]

She also had strong feelings about alcohol abuse. In many of her columns she referred to the problems caused by drunks who appeared at the doorway of the Catholic Worker house. They were often violent, they vomited all over the house, they were unruly and unreasonable in their demands. She never said that the Catholic Worker should not care for them; indeed, she saw value in the workers having to deal with such people. But these experiences convinced her of the dangers of strong drink. She wrote in her column in 1966, "We live in the midst of the tragedy drink has caused, and to use the most difficult but the only potent means to help, inflict suffering on ourselves by sacrificing this little enjoyment [alcohol], put to death that bit of self that demands this indulgence and justifies it as being harmless. I cannot believe that people are so captivated by drink that they will not give up their own harmless indulgence for the sake of others around them. It must be that they do not have faith in the weapons of the spirit or recognize their power." She concluded with a prayer, "Father, I love my brother and I love you. I want to offer you a sacrifice, and beg you in return to send Arthur or Louis the grace to overcome the most dangerous failing they suffer from."[69]

There were other moral concerns that caused her personal agony. War was one of the greatest immoralities for her. During the war in Vietnam she wrote, "We are the rich. The works of mercy are the opposite of the works of war, feeding the hungry, sheltering the homeless, nursing the sick, visiting the prisoner. But we are destroying crops, setting fire to entire villages and to the people in them. We are not performing works of mercy but the works of war."[70]

PACIFISM

Pacifism was one of Dorothy Day's most fundamental convictions. She maintained it steadfastly, even through World War II, for which she received much abuse and condemnation. When she went to Cuba in 1962 she was criticized for showing an interest in a revolution won by violence. "Several of our editors have accused us of giving up our pacifism," she wrote. "What nonsense. We are as unalterably opposed to armed resistance and armed revolt from the admittedly intolerable conditions all through Latin America as we ever were."[71]

People who opposed her often justified their position with the story of Jesus driving the money-changers out of the temple. "Over and over again," she complained, "when I am speaking in colleges and universities, this incident is brought up. There are also many strong denunciations of the oppressor, the hypocrites, the white sepulchers, the lawyers, of all those who put heavy burdens on men's shoulders and do nothing to share them or lighten them. I can only answer in these other words of His: 'Let him who is without sin among you, cast the first stone.' The most effective action we can take is to try to conform our lives to the folly of the Cross, as St. Paul called it."[72]

Day called herself an anarchist-pacifist. She disagreed with what she thought was the nihilism of the younger generation that said that in building a new society the old must be destroyed first. That, she said, was a denial of the here and now. Her understanding of anarchism was not that, but rather the understanding that Paul had when he said that "for such there is no law." She said, "For those who live in Christ Jesus, for 'those who have put on Christ,' for those who have washed the feet of others, there is no law. They have the liberty of the children of God." Such people have no desire for domination or power or the manipulation of other people.[73]

She was often asked how she could be a Catholic, a member of a church that is so authoritarian. Her reply was that "one must follow one's own conscience first before all authority, and of course, one must inform one's conscience."[74]

In 1965 she called peace "the great issue of the day." Her major concern was the war in Vietnam because there "Souls are being lost. War is a sin against Love, against life. God is Love, and he wills that all men be saved. The whole purpose of our life is Love. Why did God create us? Because He loved us. Why do we love Him? Because He first loved us. And God so loved the world that he gave His only begotten Son to us, to show us our salvation, knowing that in the exercise of our freedom we were going to continue to crucify Him to the end of the world. We are doing it now in Vietnam, in the death of every man, woman and child. 'Inasmuch as ye have done it unto the least of these my brethren ye have done it unto me.' "[75]

Four years later she wrote, "How can we show our love by war, by the extermination of our enemies? If we are followers of Christ, there is no room for speaking of the 'just war.' We have to remember that God loves all men, that God wills all men to be saved, that indeed all men are brothers. We must love the jailer as well as the one in prison. We must do that seemingly utterly impossible thing: love our enemy."[76]

In a 1970 column she told of encountering a friend of her grandson who had served in Vietnam. He told her about the Vietcong burying thousands of people alive; he had seen the corpses. He spoke, she thought, as if she had supported the Vietcong. She concluded, "It is hard to talk to each other; the words of Christianity mean so little."[77]

She was concerned that some people in the Stop the Draft Committee coalition had repudiated nonviolence. "We cannot go along with them," Dorothy said. "It was right and necessary to take to the streets and demonstrate, but to do so with anger and contempt for police or soldier was neither right nor effective." Later she added, "Hate is a lonely thing. It is one thing to hate evil, but people are people, brothers and sisters, with one common Father. One of the prayers I say often is that verse from the psalms which begs God to deliver us from the fear of our enemies. It is fear itself which engenders hatred and violence. We have to transcend fear and seek and find another source of that energy which gives us strength to love, to grow in love."[78]

For Day, the violence in the world was a manifestation of the continuing martyrdom of Christ in Vietnam, Santo Domingo, and other places where people were at war with each other. Trying to stop war by making people aware of the suffering involved will not work, she felt, because most people are willing to face any kind of suffering if they think their cause is just. She concluded, "Unless we use the weapons of the spirit, denying ourselves and taking up our cross and following Jesus, dying with Him and rising with Him, men will go on fighting, and often from the highest motives, believing that they are fighting defensive wars for justice for others and in self-defense against present or future aggression."[79]

Dorothy Day's life came to an end during the evening of November 29, 1980. She suffered from congestive heart failure and was confined to her room for the last years of her life. She was fond of quoting Father Zossima in *The Brothers Karamazov,* "Love in practice is a harsh and dreadful thing compared to love in dreams." Her work among the poor, the destitute and the deranged reveals what a harsh and dreadful thing love can be; it can put one in the midst of terrible human suffering. Yet Dorothy Day believed that the gospel calls people to that kind of love, for it is the love of Christ.

William D. Miller, in his biography of Day, described her funeral. As her grandchildren carried the pine box that contained her body into Nativity Catholic Church in New York to be greeted by Cardinal Terrence Cooke, a demented person moved to the casket and looked at it closely with great intensity. No one stopped the person, Miller said, because it was in the wretched of the world that Dorothy Day saw God.[80]

BIBLIOGRAPHY

Books by Dorothy Day:

By Little and by Little: The Selected Writings of Dorothy Day. New York: A.A. Knopf, 1983.

The Dorothy Day Book. Springfield, Illinois: Templegate, 1982.

From Union Square to Rome. Silver Spring, Md.: Preservation of the Faith Press, 1938. Reprinted by Arno Press, 1978.

House of Hospitality. New York: Sheed and Ward, 1939.

Loaves and Fishes: The Story of the Catholic Worker Movement. San Francisco: Harper and Row, 1963.

The Long Loneliness. San Francisco: Harper and Row, 1952.

On Pilgrimage: The Sixties. New York: Curtis Books, 1972.

Therese. Springfield, Illinois: Templegate, 1979.

Books about Dorothy Day:

Aronica, Michele Teresa, *Beyond Charismatic Leadership: The New York Catholic Worker Movement.* New Brunswick: Transaction Books, 1987.

Berrigan, Daniel, "The Woman," *Portraits of Those I Love.* New York: Crossroad, 1982.

Betten, Neil, *Catholic Activism and the Industrial Worker.* Gainesville: University Presses of Florida, 1976. See Chapter 4, "The Catholic Worker Movement."

Coles, Robert, *Dorothy Day: A Radical Devotion.* Reading, Massachusetts: Addison-Wesley, 1987.

Coles, Robert, *A Spectacle Unto the World: The Catholic Worker Movement.* New York: Viking Press, 1974.

Collins, David R., *Dorothy Day: Catholic Worker.* Cincinnati: St. Anthony Messenger Press, 1981.

Ellis, Marc H., *Peter Maurin: Prophet in the Twentieth Century.* New York: Paulist Press, 1981.

Klejment, Anne, *Dorothy Day and the Catholic Worker: A Bibliography and Index.* New York: Garland, 1986.

Miller, William D., *All is Grace: The Spirituality of Dorothy Day.* Garden City, N.Y.: Doubleday, 1987.

Miller, William D., "Dorothy Day," *Saints Are Now,* edited by John J. Delaney. Garden City, N.Y.: Doubleday, 1983.

Miller, William D., *Dorothy Day: A Biography.* San Francisco: Harper and Row, 1982.

Miller, William D., *A Harsh and Dreadful Love: Dorothy Day and the Catholic Worker Movement.* New York: Liveright, 1973.

Piehl, Mel, *Breaking Bread: The Catholic Worker and the Origin of Catholic Radicalism in America.* Philadelphia: Temple University Press, 1982.

Roberts, Nancy L., *Dorothy Day and the Catholic Worker.* Albany: State University of New York Press, 1984.

Statnick, Roger Andrew, *Dorothy Day's Religious Conversion: A Study in Biographical Theology.* Ph.D. Dissertation, University of Notre Dame, 1983. Reprinted by University Microfilms, Ann Arbor, Michigan.

CHAPTER V

Dietrich Bonhoeffer

DIETRICH BONHOEFFER was one of the most controversial theologians of the twentieth century, and his thought has been interpreted in many diverse ways. He has been claimed by social activists and death-of-God theologians. Some have lifted up his condemnation of religion while others have noted his disciplined piety.

There have been many fine expositions of his theology. The emphasis here, however, will be on his spirituality which was deep and which was maintained even during the darkest days of his prison experience. While he actively participated in a conspiracy to destroy Hitler, he remained a man of prayer who read the psalms and meditated on passages from the Bible every day.

EARLY LIFE

Bonhoeffer was born on February 4, 1906, one of eight children of Karl Bonhoeffer, a distinguished psychiatrist and professor at the University of Berlin. Eberhard Bethge, Bonhoeffer's friend and biographer, described his father: "He spoke quietly and infrequently, but what he said was noted. Praise and blame were given sparingly but to the point. He gave the impression of self-control and expected the same from his children. Objectivity and balance were his distinguishing characteristics. He abhorred fancy phrases;

all the children had to express themselves pertinently and as clearly and concisely as possible, without circumlocutions."[1]

Dietrich's paternal grandmother, Julie Tafel, was something of a maverick in the family. She was a strong advocate of the emancipation of women, opposed Hitler from the very beginning, and was known to have walked past SS guards to shop in a Jewish department store that was being boycotted. His mother was the granddaughter of Karl von Hase, a famous professor of church history. While growing up in Berlin-Grunewald young Dietrich had for playmates the children of Adolf von Harnack, one of the best known liberal theologians and historians of doctrine, and Hans Delbruck, a distinguished historian. The influence of family and friends began to mold Dietrich's character and intellect.

THEOLOGICAL STUDENT

Bonhoeffer surprised his family by choosing a career in theology, although his father put no pressure on him to enter any particular field. He later wrote to Dietrich, "When you made up your mind to study theology, I sometimes could not help thinking that it would be a pity for you to have the quiet, uneventful life of a minister, such as I knew my Swabian uncles had. As far as its being uneventful is concerned, I was greatly mistaken. I had no conception, with my scientific background, that nowadays there would be such a crisis in the ecclesiastical sphere too."[2]

Bonhoeffer began his academic studies at the University of Tübingen. This was his first step toward independence of the domination of his parents, but he corresponded with them frequently and asked their advice on the decisions he would have to make about lectures, student life and books. He joined the Hedgehogs, an old student fraternity founded in 1871 that had once numbered Rudolf Bultmann among its members. The fraternity filled a need for friendships and company, but Bonhoeffer left it in 1933 after it inserted the "Aryan clause" in its constitution.

Bonhoeffer had a strong interest in the academic study of theology, but no serious commitment to the church at this stage in his life. He attended lectures on philosophy, studied textual criticism, became involved in general studies outside his field, and took part in debates on social and political issues.

For his eighteenth birthday, Bonhoeffer's parents gave him a trip to Rome which had an enormous influence on his thinking. He found himself in St. Peter's on Easter and realized how provincial, nationalistic and narrow-minded was his own German Lutheran Church. He had a new sense of the universality of the church which would eventually manifest itself in wide-ranging ecumenical involvements.

He returned from Rome in June 1924 and enrolled in the University of Berlin where he would complete his studies. The university had a reputation for liberalism, and among its faculty were some of the most important scholars in Europe: Adolph von Harnack, Karl Holl and Reinhold Seeberg. In the winter of 1924–25 Bonhoeffer began to read Karl Barth. It would be years before he could have personal contact with Barth, but he began to see the church as a manifestation of revelation. Some of the professors whom Bonhoeffer heard lecture with appreciation were later expelled from Berlin by Hitler.

In 1927 Bonhoeffer presented his dissertation to the theological faculty in Berlin. Written under the direction of Reinhold Seeberg it was an attempt at a sociological theology of the church. When it was published under the title *The Communion of Saints,* it attracted no audience at all. It was not until *The Cost of Discipleship* and his prison letters appeared that people began to read it.

Theological students in Germany were required to do some practical parish work during their training. Bonhoeffer therefore took over the children's service in the Lutheran church in Grunewald. He enjoyed the work and, in addition to the church service, took the children on outings, invited them home, and held discussion groups with the older ones.

In February 1928 Bonhoeffer moved to Barcelona where he became an assistant pastor in a church serving the German Protestants who lived there. He enjoyed his parish work, but missed the lively theological discussion of Berlin.

His practical experience requirement completed, Bonhoeffer returned to Berlin in the spring of 1929. Although he seemed more attracted to the parish than academic life, he decided to qualify himself for university lecturing. He said, "I feel that academic work will not hold me for long. But I do think that as thorough an academic grounding as possible is all important."[3] He was required to present a thesis to qualify himself for teaching, and his was a small book called *Act and Being.* Here Bonhoeffer discussed, among other things, what it means to be "in Christ." The Christian, he wrote, is one who "lives only in the contemplation of Christ. This is the gift of faith, that man no longer looks on himself but on salvation alone, which has come to him from without. He finds himself in Christ because he is already in Christ from the fact of seeking himself there."[4] A few pages later he said, "Being in Christ is being turned to Christ, and this is possible only through 'being already' in the communion of Christ."[5]

On July 31, 1930 Bonhoeffer presented his inaugural lecture on the subject "The Question of Man in Contemporary Philosophy and Theology." He had now completed his examinations for ordination, but had to wait a year and a half until he reached age twenty-five to actually receive orders. In the interim he decided to visit America and spend a year studying at Union Theological Seminary in New York City.

Superintendent Max Diestel, Bonhoeffer's superior in the church, was a man of ecumenical orientation and strongly influenced by American theology and church life. He persuaded Bonhoeffer to accept a Sloane Fellowship at Union for a year's study. On September 5, 1930 he sailed for New York. Here for the first time he encountered ecumenical Christianity. In a letter to Erwin Sutz, Bonhoeffer said, "This evening I'm going to Washington, to take part in the Federal Council from the beginning. On Thursday I want to take in something of the Home Mission Council."[6]

In addition to his studies Bonhoeffer spoke and preached a number of times in America. He had one sermon that was used often, occasionally revised during the course of the year. In it he discussed the horrors of World War I. While he would not accept the statement in the Treaty of Versailles that the war was entirely the fault of Germany he did say, "Before the war we lived too far from God; we believed too much in our own power, in our almightiness and righteousness. We attempted to be a strong and good people, but we were too proud of our endeavour, we felt too much satisfaction with our scientific, economic and social progress, and we identified this progress with the coming of the Kingdom of God. We felt too happy and complacent in this world; our souls were too much at home in this world. Then the great disillusionment came. We saw the impotence and the weakness of humanity, we were suddenly awakened from our dream, we recognized our guiltiness before God and we humbled ourselves under the mighty hand of God."[7]

He then described the horrors of war, the enormous numbers of deaths and the starvation that threatened so many Germans. Now there was added the terrible burden of war debts. Finally, he concluded, "As a Christian minister I think that just here is one of the greatest tasks for our church: to strengthen the work of peace in every country in the whole world. It must never happen that a Christian people fights against a Christian people, brother against brother, since both have one Father."[8]

At the end of his year in New York he prepared a report for the church authorities in Germany. He was impressed by student life in dormitories where the emphasis was overwhelmingly on community. This had a certain leveling effect, he said, so that "there is little intellectual competition and little intellectual ambition." The seminars became friendly exchanges of opinion rather than opportunities for serious criticism. The major difference between American seminaries and European universities, he said, was that students do not learn to work independently in America. "Thus the intellectual preparation is extraordinarily thin."

His biggest complaint was the students' lack of interest in the whole field of theology. Everything seemed to him to be oriented toward practicality, either in ethics or in the work of the pastor. "The lack of seriousness with which the students here speak of God and the world is, to say the least, extremely surprising for us." In fact, he said that the only one on the faculty with any concern at all

114

about "the question of the church's message" was Harry Emerson Fosdick, and his orientation was basically humanistic. The stress on method "betrays the dwindling of content," he felt.

"The theological atmosphere of the Union Theological Seminary," Bonhoeffer concluded, "is accelerating the process of the secularization of Christianity in America. Its criticism is directed essentially against the fundamentalists and to a certain extent also against the radical humanists of Chicago; it is healthy and necessary. But there is no sound basis on which one can rebuild after demolition. It is carried away with the general collapse. A seminary in which it can come about that a large number of students laugh out loud in a public lecture at the quoting of a passage from Luther's *De servo arbitrio* on sin and forgiveness because it seems to them comic has evidently completely forgotten what Christian theology by its very nature stands for."[9]

In 1931 Bonhoeffer returned to Germany to become a university lecturer, a post from which he was removed in 1936 by the Nazi minister of education. He gave lectures and seminars, preached and served as a chaplain to students and as assistant pastor of a church. Now, for the first time, he became deeply involved in the ecumenical movement.

Before actually beginning his teaching duties he went to Bonn to hear Karl Barth lecture for three weeks. He had personal contact with Barth in discussion groups and visits in his home. He wrote to a friend, "I have been impressed even more by discussions with him than by his writings and his lectures. For he is really all there. I have never seen anything like it before and wouldn't have believed it possible."[10] His major problem with Barth's theology was what Bonhoeffer believed to be an overemphasis on eschatology that would blunt the importance of ethics, especially the peace commandment of the gospel.

During Bonhoeffer's visit to the United States the National Socialist Party had grown from insignificance to an important force in German politics. In October 1931 he wrote a letter to his friend Erwin Sutz expressing his feelings at the change that had taken place during his absence. "The outlook is really exceptionally grim. There is in fact no one in Germany who can see ahead even a little way. People, generally, are under the very definite impression that they are standing at a tremendous turning point in world history." He was concerned about the economic problems of inflation, unemployment and hunger. "Economic experts tell me," he said, "that it looks as though we are being driven at a tremendous rate towards a goal which no one knows and no one can avoid. Will our church survive yet another catastrophe, one wonders, will that not really be the end unless we become something completely different? Speak, live completely differently? But how?" He concluded the letter by raising the question, "What's the use of everyone's theology?"[11]

ECUMENICAL ACTIVITY

Bonhoeffer's early opinions about the ecumenical movement were not very positive. Bishop Nathan Söderblom of Sweden, who had influenced Hammarskjöld so much, had called together an ecumenical conference on Life and Work in Stockholm in 1925. Although a number of Berlin professors had been involved, Bonhoeffer regarded the whole effort as theologically unsatisfactory. Now, however, his outlook changed. His superintendent, Max Diestel, encouraged him to attend the World Alliance Conference in Cambridge, September 1931, as a representative of Germany. Bonhoeffer returned holding the position of secretary for youth work in central and northern Europe. German theological professors opposed the conference because of their nationalistic feelings. Paul Althaus and Emanuel Hirsch published a statement saying that understanding and cooperation with other Christian groups was impossible so long as others "conduct against us policies lethal for our nation."[12] This, however, did not diminish Bonhoeffer's enthusiasm.

His first efforts were directed toward developing an ecumenical theology while others in the movement simply wanted to pass resolutions. "The Church," he said, "must here and now be able concretely to speak the word of God, the word of power, from its own knowledge of the matter; if it does not, it is saying something different and human, a word of impotence."[13]

The youth program of the World Alliance in which Bonhoeffer was involved was united with that of Life and Work, the Sölderholm movement. It was in this work that Bonhoeffer met G.K.A. Bell, the bishop of Chichester in England, president of Life and Work. This was to be an important contact for Bonhoeffer during the tense days of the conspiracy against Hitler.

UNIVERSITY LECTURING

During this time Bonhoeffer was still lecturing at the University of Berlin. His students were sometimes shocked at behavior not typical of a German professor. For example, he offered prayers in the lecture room. He discussed the subject of peace with deep conviction before students who were, according to Bethge, "overwhelmingly Nazi sympathizers." He complained that war blinds people to revelation and insisted that "the next war must be outlawed."[14]

One of the duties given Bonhoeffer was to be chaplain at the Technical University in Charlottenburg. Although he worked earnestly at it, the effort did not succeed, and the appointment was not continued. Another task assigned to him was the instruction of an unusually unruly confirmation class in Wedding, a workers' section of Berlin. Bonhoeffer gave himself to these young people. When the usual methods of teaching did not work he told them stories from the Bible, gave them Christmas presents and took them on outings.

On January 30, 1933 Hitler came to power in Germany, and Bonhoeffer's life took on a new character. In the previous year he had said in a sermon, "We should not be surprised if the time comes for our church too, when the blood of martyrs will be called for."[15] He could not know at the time, of course, that this statement would be prophetic for his own life.

Now his own Christian life began to develop in new ways. He

took up the study of the sermon on the mount, the interpretation of which would later form the heart of his book *The Cost of Disciple-ship*. He now attended church regularly. He developed what Bethge called a disciplined *praxis pietatis* which included meditating daily on a passage of scripture. He wrote to a friend, "I discovered the Bible for the first time. . . . I know that at that time I turned the doctrine of Jesus Christ into something of personal advantage to myself. . . . It is from this that the Bible, and especially the Sermon on the Mount, set me free. Since then everything has altered. . . . It was a great liberation. It became clear to me that the life of a servant of Jesus Christ should belong to the Church. . . . Then came the 1933 crisis, which strengthened me in my conviction. Now my concern was the renewal of the Church and the ministry. Suddenly the Christian pacifism, which I had opposed passionately only a short time before, seemed to me self-evident. And so it went on, step by step."[16]

GROWING OPPOSITION

As soon as Hitler came to power Bonhoeffer began to protest. On February 1, 1933 Bonhoeffer spoke on Berlin Radio on "The Younger Generation's Changed View of the Concept of Führer." Obviously, much of the speech had been written before the Nazi victory of January 30, but it could not have been more prophetic for the occasion. Bonhoeffer warned that if a leader should "allow himself to succumb to the wishes of those he leads, who will always seek to turn him into their idol, then the image of the leader will gradually become the image of the 'misleader.' This is the leader who makes an idol of himself and his office, and who thus mocks God."[17] Before these words could be finished Bonhoeffer was cut off the air. However, he later had the entire script published.

The nature of the times can be seen in a letter he wrote to Erwin Sutz in April of 1933 in which he said, "The fact that I no longer write about conditions today is because, as you know, letters cannot be regarded as private at the present time."[18]

On April 7, 1933 Hitler imposed the notorious "Aryan

Clauses" which prohibited those of Jewish origin or married to Jews from holding office in state or church. While German Christians accepted the rulings on the grounds that the German church should be truly German, Bonhoeffer and others spoke out strongly against them. Karl Barth, for example, said that any church leadership who accepted the principles of the Aryan Clauses must be told, "Here you are no longer the church of Christ!"[19] Bonhoeffer himself wrote a carefully reasoned theological treatise on "The Church and the Jewish Question." His opposition here was not based on politics or humanitarianism, but theology. At this point he maintained the Lutheran belief that the state must be obeyed. However, the church must "continually ask the state whether its action can be justified as legitimate action of the state, i.e., as action which leads to law and order, and not to lawlessness and disorder. It will have to put this question quite clearly today in the matter of the Jewish question." Beyond this, the church can aid the victims of state action. If necessary, however, the church "is not just to bandage the victims under the wheel, but to put a spoke in the wheel itself. Such action would be direct political action, and is only possible and demanded when the church sees the state fail in its function of creating law and order."[20]

As far as church life was concerned, Bonhoeffer said, "What is at stake is by no means the question whether our German members of congregations can still tolerate church fellowship with the Jews. It is rather the task of Christian preaching to say: here is the church, where Jew and German stand together under the Word of God; here is the proof whether a church is still the church or not. No one who feels unable to tolerate church fellowship with Christians of Jewish race can be prevented from separating himself from this church fellowship. But it must be made clear to him with the utmost seriousness that he is thus loosing himself from the place on which the church of Christ stands."[21] When Bonhoeffer presented this paper at a ministers' meeting in April 1933, some of the men walked out.

In the following weeks groups of ministers formulated "confessions" which attempted to explain what the old German confessions meant for the church in 1933. Bonhoeffer had a dominant hand in the preparation of the Bethel Declaration of 1933 which said, in part, "No nation can ever be commissioned to avenge on the Jews the murder at Golgotha." With reference to Christians of Jewish descent it said, "We oppose the attempt to deprive the German Evangelical church of its promise by the attempt to change it into a national church of Christians of Aryan descent."[22]

The Aryan Clause problem was not the major difficulty, however. The condition of the German Evangelical Church was more serious even than that. The Nazi sympathizers in the church were known as the German Christians, and they moved to take over the church. In June 1933 the general superintendents of the church in Prussia were removed. Hitler's adviser on church affairs, Ludwig Muller, an army chaplain, was nominated by the German Christians as their candidate for Reich bishop. His election would simply mean Nazi control of the church. Bonhoeffer, along with Martin Niemöller and Gerhard Jacobi, pastor of Kaiser Wilhelm Memorial Church in Berlin, spoke out against Muller, but he was elected by a large majority. Bonhoeffer suggested in vain to his fellow ministers that they should leave the church because it was now heretical.

Meanwhile, Bonhoeffer was working with Niemoller to assist German pastors who suffered because of the Aryan Clause. This result was the formation of the Pastors' Emergency League. A "Declaration" was sent to ministers which said, "According to the confession of our church, the teaching office of the church is bound up with a call to the ministry of the church and with that call alone. The 'Aryan Clauses' of the new enactment concerning offices in the church puts forward a principle which contradicts this basic clause of the confession." The declaration concluded, "Anyone who gives his assent to a breach of the confession thereby excludes himself from the community of the church. We therefore demand that this law, which separates the Evangelic Church of the Old Prussian Union from the Christian church, be repealed forthwith." It was signed by Bonhoeffer and Niemoller.[23]

Bonhoeffer, however, was discouraged over the lack of a strong response to his opposition to the German Christians. He could not understand why people were so timid when there was so much at stake. He began to think that perhaps he ought to withdraw from the leadership of the struggle, even though such with-drawal was contrary to his personality. In July 1933 he was given the opportunity of serving two German congregations in London, the German Evangelical Congregation in Sydenham, whose members were businessmen, and the German Reformed Congrega-tion of St. Paul in the East End, a congregation of tradesmen. After agonizing over the decision he finally decided to go. He served the churches faithfully for a year and a half.

In October 1933 he wrote to Karl Barth about the choice. Explaining why he had not written Barth earlier for advice Bon-hoeffer said, "I knew I would have to do what you told me and I wanted to remain free; so I simply withdrew myself. I know now that that was wrong, and that I must ask you to forgive me."[24] Barth replied, "I cannot honestly tell you anything but 'Hurry back to your post in Berlin.' "[25]

While Bonhoeffer carried out his pastoral duties in London faithfully, he spent his free time developing ecumenical contacts and working in the German church struggle. He returned to Berlin every few weeks.

Meanwhile, in Germany important events were taking place in the church. In May 1934 there took place the famous Confessing Synod at Barmen. Attended by one hundred and thirty-four dele-gates from Protestant churches in Germany, the synod adopted the Barmen Declaration drafted by Karl Barth which contained six points against the German Christians. The first clause stated, "We reject the false doctrine that the Church should acknowledge, as the source of its message over and above God's Word, any other events, powers, figures and truths as divine revelation."[26] This marked the beginning of the Confessing Church in Germany. Another synod was held in Dahlen in October 1934 to set up the organizational structure of the Confessing Church. Niemoller acted as host for a provisional church administration consisting of a council of brethren and an executive council.

Bonhoeffer's efforts were now directed at getting the ecumeni-cal movement to recognize the Confessing Church as a legitimate and separate body from the Nazi church of the German Christians. His success was mixed. One of his strongest supporters, however, was G.K.A. Bell, Anglican bishop of Chichester in England, who was also president of the Ecumenical Council for Life and Work. He was greatly impressed with Bonhoeffer and became a leading advocate of the Confessing Church. Under his influence Bonhoeffer and Prases Karl Kock, head of the Confessing Synod, were made members of the Ecumenical Council. However, the Reich Church was not excluded as Bonhoeffer had hoped. In a letter to a friend Bonhoeffer said, "Hitler has shown himself very clearly for what he is and the Church ought to realize with whom it has to reckon."[27]

PREACHER'S SEMINARY

Now Bonhoeffer turned to what was to be a very important and satisfying work for him. In 1935 the Confessing Church opened a number of seminaries for the training of its ministers. In the Evangelical Church, seminary involved only a few months of training, taken after a university education was completed and before final examinations for ordination. Bonhoeffer himself avoided such studies because of his thesis for university teaching. He regarded the whole seminary effort as a waste of time, primarily because the schools were poorly staffed in comparison to the universities. Now, however, the German church situation put this brief period of training in a whole new light.

Bonhoeffer was asked by the Emergency Church Government of the Confessing Church to head the seminary in Pomerania. He began in April 1935 with twenty-five ordinands in Zingst, but soon moved to Finkenwalde where the operation was set up in a house in a very makeshift way. Beds, books and food had to be asked for, and Bonhoeffer brought his own personal library for the students to use.

After his first summer's work he wrote, "The summer of 1935 has been the most fulfilled time of my life."[28] Bonhoeffer's own personal impact on the young men in the seminary was enormous. He gave them his time freely and developed deep friendships. Many of them would later be killed in the war. However, they did not always agree with or appreciate Bonhoeffer's views. For example, they had difficulty understanding why their teacher felt that Christian discipleship might mean refusing military service. It was during this period that Bonhoeffer wrote *The Cost of Discipleship, Life Together* and *Psalms: The Prayer Book of the Bible.*

The Cost of Discipleship, first published in 1937 under the title *Nachfolge*, is probably Bonhoeffer's best known and most widely read book. The rise of Nazism and its success in taking over Germany caused Bonhoeffer to reflect deeply on the meaning of Christian discipleship. He knew that risk taking was called for. The main thrust of this book was an attack on what he called "cheap grace." The first sentence of the book states, "Cheap grace is the deadly enemy of our Church." Then he added, "We are fighting today for costly grace."[29] Bonhoeffer believed passionately in the Lutheran doctrine of justification by grace and faith, but he felt that the reception of grace must lead to new life. "It is imperative," he said, "for the Christian to achieve renunciation, to practice self-effacement, to distinguish his life from the life of the world. He must let grace be grace indeed, otherwise he will destroy the world's faith in the free gift of grace."[30]

"Cheap grace" was defined by Bonhoeffer as "the preaching of forgiveness without requiring repentance, baptism without church discipline, Communion without confession, absolution without personal confession. Cheap grace is grace without discipline, grace without the cross, grace without Jesus Christ, living and incarnate." By contrast, costly grace, he said, "is costly because it calls us to follow, and it is grace because it calls us to follow Jesus Christ. It is costly because it costs a man his life, and it is grace because it gives a man the only true life. It is costly because it condemns sin, and grace because it justifies the sinner. Above all, it is costly because it cost God the life of his Son . . . and what has cost God much cannot be cheap with us. Above all, it is grace because God did not reckon his Son too dear a price to pay for our life, but delivered him up for us. Costly grace is the incarnation of God."[31]

The Christian needs to know what the demands of discipleship are. "In the last resort, what we want to know is not, what would this or that man, or this or that Church, have of us, but what Jesus Christ himself wants of us. When we go to the church and listen to the sermon, what we want to hear is his Word."[32]

It was wrong, Bonhoeffer felt, to think that the Christian life is a matter of believing correct doctrine. Actually, it is a matter of obeying Christ. Jesus, he said, proclaimed a discipleship which liberates people from "man-made dogmas, from every burden and oppression, from every anxiety and torture which afflicts the conscience. If they follow Jesus, men escape from the hard yoke of their own laws, and submit to the kindly yoke of Jesus Christ." However, Bonhoeffer insisted that this does not mean ignoring the seriousness of Christ's commands, for "we only achieve perfect liberty and enjoy fellowship with Jesus when his command, his call to absolute discipleship, is appreciated in its entirety. Only the man who follows the command of Jesus single-mindedly, and unresistingly lets his yoke rest upon him, finds his burden easy, and under its gentle pressure receives the power to persevere in the right way. The command of Jesus is hard, unutterably hard, for those who try to resist it. But for those who willingly submit, the yoke is easy, and the burden is light." And, Bonhoeffer believed, "Jesus asks nothing of us without giving us the strength to perform it. His commandment never seeks to destroy life, but to foster, strengthen and heal it."[33]

It is impossible to predict, as Bonhoeffer understood it, where the road to discipleship will lead us, and that is part of the risk. "Only Jesus Christ, who bids us follow him, knows the journey's end. But we do know that it will be a road of boundless mercy. Discipleship means joy."[34]

In *The Cost of Discipleship* Bonhoeffer described the secularization of the church that took place when persecution ended and the world became more "Christianized." Grace then became a common property, offered without any cost. The one exception he noted was the monastic movement. "Here on the outer fringe of the Church was a place where the older vision was kept alive. Here men still remembered that grace costs, that grace means following Christ. Here they left all they had for Christ's sake, and endeavoured daily to practice his rigorous commands. Thus monasticism became a living protest against the secularization of Christianity and a cheapening of grace."[35]

Unfortunately, the Catholic Church treated monasticism as the achievement of a few that most people could not be expected to accomplish. The church developed what Bonhoeffer called a "fatal conception of the double standard," rather than teaching that the radical demands of discipleship were directed at every Christian.[36]

Bonhoeffer felt that Martin Luther restored the idea of costly grace. One follows Jesus by living in the world and by being obedient in one's daily vocation. "Only in so far as the Christian's secular calling is exercised in the following of Jesus does it receive from the gospel new sanction and justification."[37] Bonhoeffer said that "the only man who has the right to say that he is justified by grace alone is the man who has left all to follow Christ."[38]

Unfortunately, Lutheranism after Luther tended to make grace available on cheap terms. "We justified the world, and condemned as heretics those who tried to follow Christ. The result was that a nation became Christian and Lutheran, but at the cost of true discipleship. The price it was called upon to pay was all too cheap. Cheap grace had won the day."[39]

That policy resulted in the collapse of the organized church under Nazism. "We gave away the word and sacrament wholesale, we baptized, confirmed and absolved a whole nation unasked and without condition. Our humanitarian sentiment made us give that which was holy to the scornful and unbelieving. We poured forth unending streams of grace. But the call to follow Jesus in the narrow way was hardly ever heard."[40] Now, under the presence of Nazism, Bonhoeffer realized that "it is becoming clearer every day that the most urgent problem besetting our Church is this: How can we live the Christian life in the modern world?"[41]

How does one become a disciple? What is one to do? "Discipleship," wrote Bonhoeffer, "means adherence to Christ, and, because Christ is the object of that adherence, it must take the form of discipleship." We are not talking here about an abstract christology, but an actual relationship with Jesus Christ. "Christianity without the living Christ is inevitably Christianity without discipleship, and Christianity without discipleship is always Christianity without Christ."[42]

First, one is called to a new situation. Responding to the call to discipleship means leaving the past behind, dropping one's previous existence. This act places one in a situation where faith is possible. If a person refuses and wants to stay behind, in the past, he does not learn how to believe. Putting oneself in a new situation, however, "brings the disciple into fellowship with Jesus which will be victorious." In other words, one must be obedient, "for faith is only real when there is obedience, never without it, and faith only becomes faith in the act of obedience." Obedience is both the consequence and the presupposition of faith. "Only the obedient believe. If we are to believe, we must obey a concrete command. Without this preliminary step of obedience, our faith will only be pious humbug, and lead us to the grace which is not costly. Everything depends on the first step."[43]

Bonhoeffer gave some advice to pastors. When people tell their pastor that they cannot believe, this is a sign of deliberate disobedience. It is wrong to offer sympathy or consolation. Rather, the pastor should say, "You are disobedient, you are trying to keep some part of your life under control. That is what is preventing you from listening to Christ and believing in his grace. You cannot believe because you are willfully disobedient. Somewhere in your heart you are refusing to listen to his call."[44] The devil will tell a person to keep on posing problems to escape the necessity of obedience. "But the Christ whom the Scriptures proclaim is in every word he utters one who grants faith to those only who obey."[45]

Bonhoeffer was careful to point out that he is not talking about salvation by good works or a doctrine of human merit. "Obedience to the call of Jesus never lies within our own power."[46] Putting ourselves in a situation where faith is possible is "not an offer which we can make to Jesus, but always his gracious offer to us." Beyond that, "salvation through following Jesus is not something we men can achieve for ourselves—but with God all things are possible."[47]

For Bonhoeffer, the Christian life, among other things, is a life of prayer and asceticism. That is one of the signs that grace is costly.

"To deny oneself," he said, "is to be aware only of Christ and no more of self, to see only him who goes before and no more the road which is too hard for us."[48] He wrote more prophetically than he knew when he said, "To endure the cross is not a tragedy; it is the suffering which is the fruit of an exclusive allegiance to Jesus Christ. When it comes, it is not an accident, but a necessity."[49] This would turn out to be a perfect description of the last years of Bonhoeffer's own life. At this point we find what may be the most frequently quoted sentence in *The Cost of Discipleship,* "When Christ calls a man, he bids him come and die."[50]

The Christian, said Bonhoeffer, must endure several kinds of suffering. The first is that suffering which results from abandoning attachment to the world.[51] Another is the suffering caused by temptation and bearing the sins of others.[52] There is the suffering of solitude when one is forced to stand before Christ alone and respond to the call of discipleship. This solitary experience is so frightening that people tend to seek refuge in the society of others and a material environment. But this only serves to protect them from having to make a decision.[53] "Suffering, then, is the badge of true discipleship."[54] But Bonhoeffer reminded his readers that "the acts of the early Christian martyrs are full of evidence which shows how Christ transfigures his own at the hour of their mortal agony by granting them the unspeakable assurance of his presence. In the hour of the cruellest torture they bear for his sake, they are made partakers of the perfect joy and bliss of fellowship with him."[55]

Approximately one-third of *The Cost of Discipleship* is an exposition of the sermon on the mount. In the discussion of Matthew 6 Bonhoeffer dealt specifically with prayer and asceticism. The fact that Jesus had to teach his disciples to pray, said Bonhoeffer, was an indication that prayer is not a natural activity. "Christian prayer," Bonhoeffer said, "presupposes faith, that is, adherence to Christ. He is the one and only Mediator of our prayers. We pray at his command, and to that word Christian prayer is always bound."[56]

For Bonhoeffer, prayer was not a good work nor was it a matter of asking God for things. The point of it is making contact with God, knowing God. God already knows human needs. "This is what gives Christian prayer its boundless confidence and its joyous certainty. It matters little what form of prayer we adopt or how many words we use. What matters is the faith which lays hold on God and touches the heart of the Father who knew us long before we came to him."[57]

True prayer is interior and hidden. It "is the supreme instance of the hidden character of the Christian life. It is the antithesis of self-discipline. When men pray, they have ceased to know themselves and know only God whom they call upon. Prayer does not aim at any direct effect on the world; it is addressed to God alone, and therefore the perfect example of undemonstrative action."[58]

It is always tempting to become the spectator of one's own prayer. Even in solitude one can put on a nice show and congratulate oneself on praying so well. The only way to avoid this problem is "by letting Christ alone reign in our hearts, by surrendering our wills completely to him, by living in fellowship with Jesus and by following him. Then we can pray that his will may be done, the will of him who knows our needs before we ask. Only then is our prayer certain, strong and pure."[59]

Bonhoeffer believed that Jesus assumed his disciples would fast. Exercising self-control, Bonhoeffer believed, was an essential feature of Christian living. It made disciples more ready to do what God wanted. Fasting was a discipline against self-indulgence. Without self-discipline people became dominated by the flesh and it was difficult to prepare for the service of Christ. Abstemiousness by the Christian showed the world the differences between its own life and the Christian life.

Exterior discipline, then, was required for the disciple. Human effort, of course, would not by itself destroy the will of the flesh, but the well-disciplined Christian "is more clearly aware than other men of the rebellious and perennial pride of the flesh, he is conscious of his sloth and self-indulgence and knows that his arrogance must be eradicated." Bonhoeffer knew that daily self-discipline was necessary. "Only so can the flesh learn the painful lesson that it has no rights of its own. Regular daily prayer is a great help here, and so is daily meditation on the Word of God, and every kind of bodily discipline and asceticism."[60]

The flesh will resist any kind of discipline. One may resist it by saying that "evangelical liberty" means one does not have to do it. "We forget that discipline means estrangement from the world, and we forget the real joy and freedom which are the outcome of a devout rule of life. Any objection to asceticism is wrong," said Bonhoeffer. The Lutheran tradition was that all one needs is faith, but Bonhoeffer felt that this failed to recognize that "the life of faith is nothing if not an unending struggle of the spirit with every available weapon against the flesh. How is it possible to live the life of faith when we grow weary of prayer, when we lose our taste for reading the Bible, and when sleep, food and sensuality deprive us of the joy of communion with God?"[61]

Bonhoeffer rejected the idea that human suffering is in any way an imitation of Christ's suffering. That is "a godless ambition." There is no way one can do what the suffering of Christ accomplished. The only motive for asceticism, he said, was "to equip us for better service and deeper humiliation."[62] It is not a means of salvation or a means to show others one's accomplishments.

What about the possession of earthly goods? Jesus did not despise them; he used them and disciples should use them thankfully. The goods of the world are to be used but not collected. "If he stores it up as a permanent possession, he spoils not only the gift, but himself as well, for he sets his heart on his accumulated wealth, and makes it a barrier between himself and God. Where our treasure is, there is our trust, our security, our consolations, and our God. Hoarding is idolatry."[63] Bonhoeffer insisted, "Our hearts have room only for one all-embracing devotion, and we can only cleave to one Lord. Every competitor to that devotion must be hated."[64]

Bonhoeffer wrote a good bit about participation in the body of Christ. How does one actually do that? The answer, he said, is through the sacraments of baptism and the Lord's supper. The word of preaching, while important and necessary, was insufficient to make us members of Christ's body. "Baptism incorporates us into the unity of the Body of Christ, and the Lord's Supper fosters and sustains our fellowship and communion in that Body. Baptism makes us members of the Body of Christ. The communion of the body of Christ . . . is the sign and pledge that we are 'with Christ' and 'in Christ' and that he is 'in us.' "[65] The body of Christ, Bonhoeffer believed, is a visible body. It becomes visible to the world in the congregation "gathered round the Word and Sacrament."[66]

In describing the Christian's relationship with the world Bonhoeffer did not necessarily call for monastic withdrawal. He wrote that "Christians live like other men; they get married, they mourn and rejoice, they buy their requirements and use the world for the purpose of day-to-day existence. But they have everything through Christ alone, in him and for his sake. Thus they are not bound by it. They have everything as though they had it not. They do not set their heart on possessions, but are inwardly free. That is why they are able to make use of the world without withdrawing from it altogether. And that is why they can leave the world when it becomes an impediment to discipleship."[67]

Near the end of *The Cost of Discipleship* Bonhoeffer discussed justification, one's forgiveness by the mercy of God. But there is a related gift the Christian receives, the gift of sanctification or perseverance. "Justification," he said, "is the means whereby we appropriate the saving act of God in the past, and sanctification the promise of God's activity in the future. Justification secured our entrance into fellowship and communion with Christ through the unique and final event of his death, and sanctification keeps us in that fellowship in Christ."[68] Later he said, "Sanctification means that the Christians have been judged already and that they are being preserved until the coming of Christ and are ever advancing towards it."[69]

The last chapter of *The Cost of Discipleship* is on "The Image of Christ." Bonhoeffer quoted Romans 8:29 where Paul wrote of those whom God has predestined "to be conformed to the image of his Son, in order that he might be the first-born among many brethren." Bonhoeffer exclaimed, "Here is a promise which passes all understanding. Those who follow Christ are destined to bear his image." The image of Christ, he said, has a profound effect upon one who follows him, for one cannot contemplate that image without being transformed by it. One receives the image by surrendering to Christ.[70]

One does not receive the image of Christ by trying to imitate him, for one cannot force oneself into that image. Rather, Christ himself produces that image in a person. Christ's work is not finished until he has perfected his own form in a person. One must be assimilated to the form of Christ in its entirety, the form of Christ "incarnate, crucified, and glorified."[71]

For Bonhoeffer, it was the contemplation of Christ that forms the image of Christ in a person. "If we contemplate the image of the glorified Christ, we shall be made like unto it, just as by contemplating the image of Christ crucified we are conformed to his death. We shall be drawn into his image, and identified with his form, and become a reflection of him. That reflection of his glory will shine forth in us even in this life, even as we share his agony and fear his cross."[72]

Bonhoeffer concluded, "This is what we mean when we speak of Christ dwelling in our hearts. His life on earth is not finished yet, for he continues to live in the lives of his followers. Indeed it is wrong to speak of the Christian life: we should rather speak of Christ living among us."[73]

COMMUNITY LIFE

Bonhoeffer's interest in operating the Preacher's Seminary was not just in theology. He was also interested in the development of community life, a community life that was particularly intense under Nazi rule. This is reflected in the second book written during the days at Finkenwalde, *Life Together.* Here Bonhoeffer described what community life among Christians ought to be.

As one reads Bonhoeffer's descriptions of Christ's situation in the world, one knows that they reflect the condition of the Christian under Nazism. "Jesus Christ lived in the midst of his enemies. At the end all his disciples deserted him. On the Cross he was utterly alone, surrounded by evildoers and mockers. For this cause he had come, to bring peace to the enemies of God. So the Christian, too, belongs not in the seclusion of a cloistered life but in the thick of foes. There is his commission, his work."[74]

One of the things that makes this bearable for the Christian is the presence of fellow disciples, "a source of incomparable joy and strength to the believer." But this is more than just a matter of sympathetic companionship. "The prisoner, the sick person, the Christian in exile sees in the companionship of a fellow Christian a physical sign of the gracious presence of the triune God. Visitor and visited in loneliness recognize in each other the Christ who is present in the body; they receive and meet each other as one meets the Lord."[75]

The Christian community, for Bonhoeffer, was a christocentric community. One's brothers and sisters were those who had been redeemed by Christ, freed from sin, and called to faith. Christian community is based on what people do by reason of Christ, and on what Christ has done to people.[76]

Nevertheless, the Christian community is by no means a perfect community. Human realities are there and the way those realities are faced determines the character of the community. "By sheer grace, God will not permit us to live even for a brief period in a dream world," Bonhoeffer said. "Only that fellowship which faces such disillusionment, with all its unhappy and ugly aspects, begins to be what it should be in God's sight, begins to grasp in faith the promise that is given to it. The sooner this shock of disillusionment comes to an individual and to a community the better for both. A community which cannot bear and cannot survive such a crisis, which insists upon keeping its illusion when it should be shattered, permanently loses in that moment the promise of Christian community."[77]

In *Life Together* Bonhoeffer outlined the spiritual activity of the Christian community. The day, he said, should begin with common prayer. "The deep stillness of the morning is broken first by the prayer and song of the fellowship. After the silence of night and early morning, hymns and the Word of God are more easily grasped."[78] The morning worship should include scripture reading, song and prayer. In this connection he discussed the use of the psalms as prayer. As for reading scripture, Bonhoeffer had a sense of the relatedness and the unity of the Bible. "Only in the infiniteness of its inner relationships, in the connection of Old and New Testaments, of promise and fulfillment, sacrifice and law, law and gospel, cross and resurrection, faith and obedience, having and hoping, will the full witness to Jesus Christ the Lord be perceived."[79] Bonhoeffer rejected the use of scripture as a means of finding what God wants for oneself. "It is in fact more important for us to know what God did to Israel, to His Son Jesus Christ, than to seek what God intends for us today. I find no salvation in my life history, but only in the history of Jesus Christ."[80]

Common prayer, the prayer of the community, is essential to successful community life, Bonhoeffer believed. It is a difficult part of the devotional life because this is when individuals begin to speak. The prayers that people offer in a community ought not to be their own, he said, but should be prayers of the whole fellowship. They are offered by one who shares the fellowship and ought to reflect the daily life of the fellowship. This requires watchfulness and a sensitivity to the needs of the community.

The day's work of the community should be rooted in prayer; there should be a union of prayer and work. To find the Thou of God in the it of work is what Paul called prayer without ceasing. Prayer occurs not only at scheduled times, but it is taken into the heart of one's work. "It includes the whole day, and in doing so, it does not hinder the work; it promotes it, affirms it, and lends it meaning and joy." This kind of unity gives the day order and discipline, which means that the prayer of the morning determines the day. "The organization and distribution of our time will be better for having been rooted in prayer. Decisions which our work demands will be simpler and easier when they are made, not in the fear of men, but solely in the presence of God. Even routine mechanical work will be performed more patiently when it is done with the knowledge of God and His command."[81]

Whenever it is practical, the community should observe midday prayer. "To Him alone the day belongs, and so, in the middle of the day, the Christian fellowship gathers and accepts God's invitation to come and eat. At the height of the day the Church lifts up its voice to the triune God in praise of His wonders and prayer for help and speedy redemption. At midday the heavens were darkened above the Cross of Jesus. The work of atonement was approaching its completion."[82]

At the end of the day there should be common prayer again.

While this may occur at the evening meal, Bonhoeffer felt, "It is an excellent thing if the evening devotion can be held at the actual end of the day, thus becoming the last word before the night's rest. When night falls, the true light of God's Word shines brighter for the Church. The prayer of the Psalms, a hymn, and the common prayer close the day, as they opened it."[83]

Bonhoeffer gave specific instruction for the evening prayer. It should include petitions for "the blessing, peace, and safety of all Christendom; for our congregation; for the pastor in his ministry; for the poor, wretched, and lonely; for the sick and dying; for our neighbors, for our own folks at home, and for our fellowship." It should also include petitions for forgiveness "for every wrong done to God and our brothers." Finally, noted Bonhoeffer, "in all the ancient evening prayers we are struck by the frequency with which we encounter preservation during the night from the devil, from terror, and from an evil, sudden death."[84]

The common spiritual life of the community was important to Bonhoeffer, but one chapter of *Life Together* is called "The Day Alone." Here he outlined the things the Christian does individually in fostering spiritual growth. These included the use of silence, meditation, and personal prayer.

"Silence," Bonhoeffer wrote, "is the simple stillness of the individual under the Word of God." The word of God, he believed, demands silence. "We are silent before hearing the Word because our thoughts are already directed to the Word. We are silent after hearing the Word because the Word is still speaking and dwelling within us. We are silent at the beginning of the day because God should have the first word, and we are silent before going to sleep because the last word also belongs to God. We keep silence solely for the sake of the Word, and therefore not in order to show disregard for the Word but rather to honor and receive it."[85]

This stillness and silence before the word of God will exercise its influence throughout the whole day for the Christian who takes it seriously. It produces clarification, purification and concentration. More than that, however, "silence before the Word leads to right hearing and thus also to right speaking of the Word of God at the right time." It is so essential that people living in a close community, like a family, have times of quiet. "After a time of quiet we meet others in a different and fresh way."[86]

Meditation is one of the fruitful ways to use silence. Meditation on scripture, said Bonhoeffer, "lets us be alone with the Word. And in so doing it gives us solid ground on which to stand and clear directions as to the steps we must take."[87]

He saw meditation, which he himself did daily, even while in prison, as a matter of pondering a text of scripture "on the strength of the promise that it has something utterly personal to say to us for this day and for our Christian life, that it is not only God's Word for the Church, but also God's Word for us individually. We expose ourselves to the specific word until it addresses us personally."[88] One need not meditate on every sentence in a passage. It may be that one sentence or one word will speak in such a way that one will not want to leave it. Bonhoeffer realized that it may take some time for the word of God to break through. Minds are full of thoughts, images and concerns which must first be swept aside. But if one waits patiently it will surely come and come again.

The purpose of meditation on scripture is not to discover new ideas. This would only serve to feed vanity. The point of meditation is simply to understand the word and let it penetrate and dwell. Nor should one look for extraordinary experiences. "It is here that our vanity and our illicit claims upon God may creep in and by a pious detour, as if it were our right to have nothing but elevating and fruitful experiences, as if the discovery of our own inner poverty were quite below our dignity."[89]

On the other hand, we must also recognize that in meditation "there will be times when we feel a great spiritual dryness and apathy, an aversion, even an inability to meditate." This should not be allowed to induce self-pity or self-reproach. Rather, one "must center attention on the Word alone and leave consequences to its action."[90]

Serious meditation should lead next to prayer. Bonhoeffer believed that "the most promising method of prayer is to allow oneself to be guided by the word of the Scriptures, to pray on the basis of a word of Scripture." There was a passive element in Bonhoeffer's understanding of prayer. "Prayer means nothing else," he said, "but the readiness and willingness to receive and appropriate the Word, and, what is more, to accept it in one's personal situation, particular tasks, decisions, sins, and temptations."[91]

In personal prayer one can say to God what could never be said in the common prayers of the fellowship. One may pray for "the clarification of our day, for preservation from sin, for growth in sanctification, for faithfulness and strength in our work." One can do this in faith that prayer will be heard "because it is a response to God's Word and promise."[92]

Bonhoeffer was aware of the human problems in prayer. He knew that thoughts wander and concentration breaks as one thinks about other people and problems and anxieties. But he offered some advice. "When this happens it is often a help not to snatch back our thoughts convulsively, but quite calmly to incorporate into our prayer the people and events to which our thoughts keep straying and thus in all patience return to the starting point of the meditation."[93]

If prayer had a passive aspect for Bonhoeffer, it also had an active side. The third use of silence he recommended in *Life Together* was intercession. "A Christian fellowship lives and exists by the intercession of its members for one another, or it collapses." But the most important reason for intercessory prayer, said Bonhoeffer, is that "I can no longer condemn or hate a brother for whom I pray, no matter how much trouble he causes me." In intercessory prayer such a person is transformed from an enemy to someone for whom Christ died. "To make intercession means to grant our brother the same right that we have received, namely, to stand before Christ and share in his mercy."[94]

Bonhoeffer concluded this section of *Life Together* by insisting that one should set aside a regular time for meditation, prayer and intercession. For most people, he believed, the early morning would be the best time. "We have a right to this time, even prior to the claims of other people, and we may insist upon having it as a completely undisturbed quiet time despite all external difficulties. For the pastor it is an indispensable duty and his whole ministry will depend on it. Who can really be faithful in great things if he has not learned to be faithful in the things of daily life?"[95]

There is a test for the authenticity of these spiritual exercises. Bonhoeffer knew that the Christian would spend many hours in what one might call an "unchristian environment," and these hours would reveal what has happened in the interior life. Regarding meditation, Bonhoeffer asked, "Has it transported him for a moment into a spiritual ecstasy that vanishes when everyday life returns, or has it lodged the Word of God so securely and deeply in his heart that it holds and fortifies him, impelling him to active love, to obedience, to good works? Only the day can decide."[96]

It is here that one can see a strong connection between spirituality and social action. When the presence of God is sensed in daily living through spiritual disciplines, events are seen in a new light. "We must be ready to allow ourselves to be interrupted by God. God will be constantly crossing our paths and canceling our plans by sending us people with claims and petitions. We may pass them by, preoccupied with our more important tasks, as the priest passed by the man who had fallen among thieves, perhaps—reading the Bible. When we do that we pass by the visible sign of the Cross raised athwart our path to show us that, not our way, but God's way must be done. It is part of the discipline of humility that we must not spare our hand where it can perform a service and that we do not assume that our schedule is our own to manage, but allow it to be arranged by God."[97]

PRAYING THE PSALMS

One of the most ancient practices of the Christian spiritual tradition is praying the psalms in the Old Testament. It is the foundation of monastic prayer and, in the middle ages, people who could afford them had Books of Hours which had the psalms arranged for prayer at various times of the day. Bonhoeffer, too, knew the value of praying the psalms. He discussed the practice briefly in *Life Together* and, while at Finkenwalde, wrote a small volume called *Psalms: The Prayer Book of the Bible.*

In *Life Together* Bonhoeffer called the psalter "the great school of prayer. Here one learns, first, what prayer means. It means praying according to the Word of God, on the basis of the promises. Christian prayer takes its stand on the solid ground of the revealed Word and has nothing to do with vague, self-seeking vagaries. We pray on the basis of the prayer of the true Man Jesus Christ."[98] This last statement expresses a fundamental element in Bonhoeffer's attitude toward the psalms.

He was aware that many Christians find the psalter difficult to pray. Some psalms lend themselves naturally to devotional use, but some are imprecatory, vengeful and bitter. Yet these are part of scripture and must have some meaning and usefulness for us. For Bonhoeffer, they are the psalms of Christ who knew suffering, pain and injustice. "A psalm that we cannot utter as a prayer, that makes us falter and horrifies us, is a hint to us that here Someone else is praying, not we; and the One who is here protesting his innocence, who is invoking God's judgment, who has come to such infinite depths of suffering, is none other than Jesus Christ himself."[99]

This makes the psalter "the prayer book of Jesus in the truest sense of the word." It is in the psalter that one encounters the praying Christ. When one prays the psalms one prays the prayers of Christ and, Bonhoeffer said, "because those who pray the psalms are joining in with the prayer of Jesus Christ, their prayer reaches the ears of God. Christ becomes their intercessor." Therefore, "the Psalter is the vicarious prayer of Christ for his Church."[100]

How then can one pray the imprecatory psalms? Bonhoeffer answered, "In so far as we are sinners and express evil thoughts in a prayer of vengeance, we dare not do so. But in so far as Christ is in us, the Christ who took all the vengeance of God upon himself, who met God's vengeance in our stead, who thus—stricken by the wrath of God—and in no other way, could forgive his enemies, he himself suffered the wrath that his enemies might go free—we, too, as members of this Jesus Christ, can pray these psalms, through Jesus Christ, from the heart of Jesus Christ."[101]

In the small volume *Psalms: The Prayer Book of the Bible,* Bonhoeffer faced a fact that many people who have tried to develop serious prayer lives have found, that the heart cannot pray by itself. It is frustrating to be "speechless before God, to discover that every call to him dies within itself, that heart and mouth speak an absurd language that God does not want to hear." However, if Christ "takes us with him in his prayer, if we are privileged to pray along with him, and if he lets us accompany him on his way to God and teaches us to pray, then we are free from the agony of prayerlessness. But that is precisely what Jesus Christ wants us to do. He wants us to pray with him, so that we may be confident and glad that God hears us."[102]

God has given the psalms to teach people how to pray. "We learn to speak to God because God has spoken to us and speaks to us. By means of the speech of the Father in heaven his children learn to speak with him. Repeating God's own words after him, we begin to pray with him."[103] Praying scripture meant, for Bonhoeffer, that the word that God gives people is the same word they return in prayer.

How is it possible for people and Christ to pray psalms together? Bonhoeffer answered, "It is the incarnate Son of God, who has borne every human weakness in his own flesh, who here pours out the heart to all humanity before God who stands in our place and prays for us. He has known torment and pain, guilt and death more deeply than we. Therefore it is the prayer of the human nature assumed by him which comes here before God."[104] He believed that the psalter was essential to a good prayer life. "Whenever the Psalter is abandoned, an incomparable treasure vanishes from the Christian Church. With its recovery will come unsuspected power."[105]

In the summer of 1935, when Bonhoeffer had begun his seminary, Hitler established a church ministry with Hans Kerrl as the new minister of church affairs. An effort was made to pacify the churches through the establishment of church committees made up of German Christians, neutrals, and leaders of the Confessing Church. Christians were called to take an oath which said, "We affirm the National Socialist development of our nation on the basis of race, blood and land." The Confessing Church was immediately divided. Direct disobedience to the state was more than many of its members could do, and it was reduced drastically in size. In December 1935 the government decreed that any government within the church would be illegal. This, of course, made the seminaries operated under the Council of Brethren illegal. Bonhoeffer called his students together immediately and told them they could leave. All remained. The seminary was located in such a remote place that it was not immediately troubled by the government. In two years, however, the Gestapo would close it down. Even then, Bonhoeffer continued to teach his students while they were serving in churches, spending half a week in each of two different locations. In March 1940 the Gestapo put a stop even to that, but it really did not matter as most of the students were now in the army.

The unique thing about Bonhoeffer's seminary was its intense community and spiritual life. Bonhoeffer insisted on thirty minutes of silent meditation on the Bible for himself and the students, a practice he continued in prison. He also restored the practice of personal confession. These things, he felt, formed the roots of good preaching. He was accused of being monastic and legalistic, to which he replied, "What could be legalistic about a Christian making an effort to learn what prayer is and spending a good deal of his time in learning about it?"[106]

When his first group of students completed their studies in the fall of 1935, Bonhoeffer asked several of them to stay on and form a spiritual community. They would take no vows but would follow a discipline of prayer and devotion, would take some responsibilities in nearby parishes, and would assist in the seminary. The group called itself "The House of the Brethren." It maintained a sense of continuity in a seminary where the student body changed every six months, but it was also a new form of pastorate. The experiment ended with the closing of the seminary, and an effort to restore it after the war failed.

The events surrounding the closing of the seminary produced restrictions on Bonhoeffer. He was removed from his teaching post at the university in 1936. In 1938 the Gestapo broke into a meeting of Confessing Church leaders on education and said that non-residents, including Bonhoeffer, could no longer enter Berlin. Bonhoeffer's father managed to have the order modified so Dietrich could visit his parents, but he was forever prohibited from participating in church activities in Berlin. The Bonhoeffer home in Marienburger Allee became the meeting place for many activities.

In 1940 the Reich Security Office in Berlin issued a decree that

Bonhoeffer, as well as seven other Confessing Church pastors, was not to make any public appearances or speeches in Germany and that he was to report his movements to the police regularly.

CONSPIRACY

The most controversial element in Bonhoeffer's life was his involvement in a plot to assassinate Hitler. There was certainly nothing in Lutheran tradition to support such a step. Obedience to the powers that be had always been a part of Lutheran ethics. But Bonhoeffer could not be satisfied with that. The combination of his faith and the situation within Germany moved him to take radical action. Gradually, but inexorably, he was drawn into the conspiracy.

Bishop G.K.A. Bell of England once quoted Bonhoeffer as saying, "If we claim to be Christians, there is no room for expediency. Hitler is the Antichrist. Therefore we must go on with our work and eliminate him whether he be successful or not."[107] Bonhoeffer's close friend and biographer Eberhard Bethge questioned the accuracy of this widely quoted statement. He noted that a reference to Hitler as the Antichrist did not occur in anything else Bonhoeffer wrote. In fact, Bethge remembered a conversation in which the matter was discussed and Bonhoeffer replied, "No, he is not the Antichrist; Hitler is not big enough for that; the Antichrist uses him, but he is not as stupid as that man!"[108]

Movements to overthrow Hitler were already underway in the upper echelons of the Germany military when Bonhoeffer first became involved. One of his major contacts was his own brother-in-law, Hans von Dohnanyi, who was involved in the investigation of the dismissal of General Werner Freiherr von Fritsch. Also involved were General Hans Oster, head of the military security department of Admiral Wilhelm Canaris, and General Ludwig Beck who would become a major leader in the conspiracy. As a confidant of Dohnanyi, Bonhoeffer knew about the conspiracy and thus was an accessory—a capital crime. What was his involvement to be?

At the same time Bonhoeffer was preparing for another sabbatical in the United States. With encouragement from Reinhold Niebuhr and Paul Lehman he set out from Berlin on June 2, 1939. The time spent in America was miserable. Bonhoeffer longed for news from Germany, worried about the fate of the churches, and felt that he had made a mistake in coming.

He kept a diary during his stay in New York at Union Theological Seminary. In general, he felt that American theology was fifteen to twenty years behind that in Germany. He wrote of a conversation with Henry Sloan Coffin, president of Union Seminary, and remarked how he criticized his colleagues. Bonhoeffer commented, "I don't think we can be like that at home any more. Too much binds us together, despite all the differences of opinion."[109] In the same June 13, 1939 entry Bonhoeffer said, "I do not understand why I am here, whether it was a sensible thing to do, whether the results will be worthwhile."[110] Two days later he wrote, "Since yesterday evening I haven't been able to stop thinking of Germany," and after describing an inconsequential conversation with a woman friend he claimed, "I would gladly have taken the next ship home." His major complaint, however, was: "I still hadn't found peace for Bible reading and prayer." He concluded, "I must go back within a year at the latest."[111]

Bonhoeffer was not impressed with American preaching, particularly at Riverside Church. He described the service there as "quite unbearable," and called it "a respectable, self-indulgent, self-satisfied religious celebration." The same evening, however, he attended services at Broadway Presbyterian and rejoiced that the minister preached on "our likeness with Christ." Bonhoeffer called it a "completely Biblical sermon" and liked the comments that "we are blameless with Christ" and "we are tempted like Christ." He concluded that "this will one day be a centre of resistance when Riverside Church has long since become a temple of Baal."[112]

In the diary Bonhoeffer wrote frequently of his prayer and devotional life. He always ended the day with Bible reading and prayer. In one entry he wrote of prayer as the means of staying in touch with his German brethren. "God, grant me in the next few weeks clarity about my future and keep me in the communion of prayer with the brethren," he prayed. He also commented, "It disturbs me that we do not keep the same time as Germany. It hinders and prevents prayer together."[113]

Many of the entries in his diary speak of Bonhoeffer's devotional life. For example, a June 20, 1939 entry: "Isaiah 45:19; I Peter 1:17. Today the reading speaks dreadfully harshly of God's incorruptible judgment. He certainly sees how much personal feeling, how much anxiety there is in today's decision."[114] June 21, 1939: "The reading is again so harsh: 'He will sit as a refiner of gold and silver.' (Malachi 3:3) And it is necessary. I don't know where I am. But he knows; and in the end all doings and actions will be pure and clear."[115] The June 22, 1939 entry ends with "Readings and intercessions" July 2, 1939: "Isaiah 35:10! Intercessions."[116] July 5, 1939, "The readings call for thankfulness."[117] Bonhoeffer developed a consistent discipline of prayer and Bible reading that continued even in his prison days.

Finally, after much agony, Bonhoeffer decided he must return to Germany and face all the dangers that decision implied. In a June 28, 1939 diary entry he wrote, "I cannot imagine that it is God's will for me to remain here without anything particular to do in the case of war. I must travel at the first possible opportunity."[118] Two days later he added, "If war breaks out I do not want to be here." There followed the comment, "Morning prayers by Coffin were very poor. I must take care not to be remiss with Bible reading and prayer."[119]

Finally, Bonhoeffer made his decision. He wrote a letter to Reinhold Niebuhr. "I have had the time to think and pray about my situation and that of my nation and to have God's will for me clarified. I have come to the conclusion that I have made a mistake in coming to America. I must live through this difficult period of our national history with the Christian people of Germany. I will have no right to participate in the reconstruction of Christian life in Germany after the war if I do not share in the trials of this time with my people."[120]

He sailed on July 7, 1939. Two days later he wrote in his diary, "Since I have been on ship my inner uncertainty about the future has ceased. I can think of my shortened time in America without reproaches. Reading: 'It is good for me that I was afflicted, that I might learn thy statutes' (Psalms 119:71). One of my favorite verses from my favorite psalm.''[121]

After returning to Germany Bonhoeffer and his friend Eberhard Bethge were made church visitors by the Council of Brethren of the Confessing Church. In the summer of 1940 they traveled throughout east Prussian parishes. During this time France surrendered to the Germans and Hitler seemed invincible. In the wake of this news the Gestapo raided a Bible study group Bonhoeffer was leading at a youth conference in Bloestau, near Konigsberg. Bonhoeffer was banned from public speaking as a subversive and was required to report regularly to the authorities. This problem was overcome by his brother-in-law, Dohnanyi, who arranged for him to be employed by the Abwehr, a security agency, working out of the Munich office. Not only did this give Bonhoeffer much needed protection, but it introduced him into the inner circle of the military conspiracy against Hitler. Officially, Bonhoeffer was still working for the Confessing Church, and the Abwehr expected him to use his church travels as a means of intelligence gathering.

From the point of view of the conspiracy his travels were to serve three purposes: first, to inform sympathizers of the resistance movement; second, to attempt to discover Allied peace aims; third, to ask the Allies for time to establish a new German government if Hitler was overthrown which could not be done if the Allies continued to press the war. One of Bonhoeffer's most important contacts was Bishop G.K.A. Bell of the Anglican Church.[122]

Bonhoeffer's travels and foreign contacts aroused the suspicions of the Nazis, and he and Dohnanyi were warned that they were being watched and their telephones tapped. On April 5, 1943 Bonhoeffer was arrested and taken to Tegel prison.

PRAYER LIFE IN PRISON

The first letter available from Bonhoeffer was written to his parents nine days after his arrest. He told them not to worry about him, that he was not afraid of solitude. "I am not so unused to solitude as some people would be, and it is quite as good as a turkish bath for the soul." He began to develop the spiritual discipline needed to cope with prison life. "What a great comfort Paul Gerhardt's hymns are! I am learning them off by heart. Then I have got my Bible and some books out of the library here, and enough writing paper now."[123]

On Easter Sunday, 1943 he wrote of the importance of his Easter meditations. "I want you to know that I am having a happy Easter in spite of everything. One of the great advantages of Good Friday and Easter Day is that they take us out of ourselves, and make us think of other things, of life and its meaning, and its sufferings and events."[124]

Bible reading was becoming a major part of his routine. "I read a good deal—newspapers, novels, and above all the Bible. I can't concentrate enough yet for serious work, but during Holy Week I at last managed to work through a part of the passion story which has been worrying me for a long time—the High Priestly prayer of our Lord. I have also studied some of the ethical sections of the Pauline Epistles. I spend the time before I get to sleep saying over to myself the hymns I have learnt during the day and when I wake up (about 6 AM) I like to read a few psalms and hymns, think about you all and remember that you are thinking about me."[125]

By the middle of May 1943 Bonhoeffer was well into a discipline of Bible reading. "For all my sympathy with the contemplative life, I am not a born Trappist! A temporary rule of silence may be a good thing, and Catholics tell us that the best expositions of Scripture come from the purely contemplative orders. I am reading the Bible straight through from cover to cover and have just got to the book of Job, a firm favorite of mine. I am reading the psalms daily, as I have done for years. I know them and love them more than any other book in the Bible."[126]

Whitsunday, June 14, 1943, was the occasion of a letter in which Bonhoeffer expressed his regret that he could not go to church. "Instead I followed St. John's example on the isle of Patmos and held a nice little service of my own. Every hour or so since yesterday morning I have been repeating to myself the words: 'Thou art a Spirit of joy,' and 'God grant us strength and power.'

These words are a great comfort—from Paul Gerhardt's Whitsun hymn, which I love so much."[127]

By autumn, study had become an important part of Bonhoeffer's routine. "After breakfast," he wrote in a letter dated October 13, 1943, "I read some theology, then I write until midday; in the afternoon I read, and then comes a chapter of Delbruck's *History of the World,* and some English grammar—of which I still have a lot to learn, and finally, as the mood takes me, I read or write again."[128]

At the end of the year Bonhoeffer wrote about his Christmas observance. "I lit the candles you and M. sent me and read the Christmas story and a few beautiful carols and hummed them over to myself. This helped me to think of you all and to hope that you all might enjoy an hour or two of quietness after the turbulence of the past weeks."[129]

In a letter to a friend dated November 18, 1943, Bonhoeffer told of being in a cell between two prisoners who had been condemned to death. He wrote, "During this time Paul Gerharrdt was a wonderful help, more than I could have dreamed of. So were the psalms and the Apocalypse. They helped preserve me from any serious spiritual trial. I made up my mind that it was my duty to face the worst. In this way I have become quite content about it all, and have remained so until this day." He added, "I have been reading the Bible every day, and as soon as it was possible I started on some non-theological work. I have read the Old Testament through two and a half times, and have learnt a great deal. I am trying to compile some prayers for use in prison. It's strange there don't seem to be any in existence."[130]

Bonhoeffer is known for his opposition to religiosity, although that is greatly overplayed in contemporary theology. In a November 21, 1943, letter he said, "I have found great help in Luther's advice that we should start our morning and evening prayers by making the sign of the cross. There is something objective about it, and that is what I need very badly here. Don't worry, I shan't come out of here a *homo religiosus!* On the contrary my suspicion and horror of religiosity are greater than ever. I often think of how the Israelites never uttered the name of God. I can understand that much better than I used to."[131]

146

One of the horrors of the prison experience was the constant air raids. The prisoners were often herded together into crowded bomb shelters. Bonhoeffer described one such experience in a letter of November 29, 1943. "All this time I lay in complete darkness on the floor, with little hope of coming through it all safely. Now here's the point—it led me back to prayer and to the Bible just like a child. More of that later when I see you. In more than one respect my confinement is acting like a wholesome though drastic cure."[132]

A letter written on December 18, 1943 is the most depressing in the whole collection. Bonhoeffer confessed that he had given up all hope of release. He had expected to be released the previous day, but had not been. Now, he said, "I shall probably sit here for weeks." He mused that one should do everything possible to change the course of events. If one fails, at least there is the consolation of having done everything possible. "Of course," he wrote, "not everything that happens is the will of God, yet in the last resort nothing happens without his will, i.e., through every event, however untoward, there is always a way through to God."[133]

He complained of being "terribly homesick" in prison, but concluded that he had learned something from the experience. First, he said that the greatest temptation was "to abandon the daily routine with the result that our lives become disordered." He was tempted to stay in bed after six in the morning, but, he noted, "I realize that that would have been the first stage of capitulation, and no doubt worse would have followed." Then, he believed, "the power to overcome tension, which can only come from looking the longing straight in the face, is used up, and endurance becomes even more intolerable." A second thing he learned from his experience was that people ought not to talk to strangers about their feelings, although they should be ready to listen to each other. "Above all, we should never give way to self-pity."[134]

Speculating from his cell, Bonhoeffer wrote that people ought to love God in all the blessings that God gives in life, but should not "try to be more religious than God Himself." To long for God when a man is in his wife's arms is "a lack of taste, and it is certainly not what God expects of us." When a person has found God in the joys of life, there will be many opportunities of reminding oneself that earthly pleasures are only temporary. "But everything in its season, and the important thing is to keep step with God and not get a step or two in front of Him."[135]

The most quoted and studied letter in the whole Bonhoeffer corpus is the one of April 30, 1944. By the time of this letter Bonhoeffer had been in prison for just over a year. In just under a year later he would be hanged. So this piece comes from around the mid-point of his prison stay. The letter has been interpreted in many ways. It has been seen by many as a contribution to the death of God theology. Yet the study of Bonhoeffer's total life and writings can hardly lead to this conclusion.

Bonhoeffer opened the letter by asserting that "I am sure God is about to do something which we can only accept with wonder and amazement." He revealed that he was still practicing a rather traditional form of piety: "I am so sorry I can't help you at all, except by thinking of you as I read the Bible every morning and evening, and often during the day." Nevertheless, Bonhoeffer told his friend, "You would be surprised and perhaps disturbed if you knew how my ideas on theology are taking shape." He has been speculating, he said, on what Christianity is and what Jesus Christ means for the present. He was obviously trying to understand what Christ meant for a person in a Nazi prison whose life was in danger at the hands of those who would destroy all the values of western civilization. Traditional religious formulations simply did not speak to that situation. Religion, as it had been known and understood in the past, had nothing to offer in those conditions of life. "We are proceeding toward a time of no religion at all: men as they are now simply cannot be religious anymore," Bonhoeffer wrote. Religion was "an historical and temporary form of human self-expression," and it can no longer be assumed that people are basically religious. People are now living without religion, Bonhoeffer stated, "else how is it, for instance, that this war, unlike any of those before it, is not calling forth any 'religious' reaction—what does that mean for 'Christianity'?"[136]

Bonhoeffer wondered if religion was just the garment of Christianity. If so, then what is a "religionless" Christianity, Christianity with its garments removed? This raised the question of

"How do we speak of God without religion, i.e., without the temporally influenced presuppositions of metaphysics, inwardness, and so on? How do we speak in a secular fashion of God?" Christ, he said, "is no longer an object of religion, but something quite different, indeed and in truth the Lord of the world."[137] What does that mean for worship and prayer and the spiritual life?

Religion, he wondered, may no more be a condition of salvation than circumcision was for Paul. "Freedom from circumcision is at the same time freedom from religion." He doubted the value of using God to solve problems on the borders of human existence, because as humanity pushes those borders out further God becomes less necessary. "I should like to speak of God not on the borders of life but at its centre, not in weakness, but in strength, not, therefore, in man's suffering and death but in his life and prosperity. On the borders it seems to me better to hold our peace and leave the problems unsolved." Bonhoeffer concluded by affirming that "God is the 'beyond' in the midst of our life. The Church stands not where human powers give out, on the borders, but in the centre of the village." He ended the letter by saying, "The outward aspect of this religionless Christianity, the form it takes, is something to which I am giving much thought."[138]

A few days later, May 5, Bonhoeffer stated his belief that people in the world were no longer concerned with the matter of individual salvation. That being the case, he said, "I am thinking over the problem at present how we may reinterpret in the manner 'of the world'—in the sense of the Old Testament and John 1:14 —the concepts of repentance, faith, justification, rebirth, sanctification and so on."[139]

The self-denying life which Bonhoeffer was forced to live in prison must have affected his spirituality. However, he was no rigid ascetic. He believed that while God wanted to be loved by people with their whole hearts, they were not to diminish their earthly affections for each other. "Even the Bible can find room for the Song of Songs, and one could hardly have a more passionate and sensual love than is there portrayed. It is a good thing that that book is included in the Bible as a protest against those who believe that Christianity stands for the restraint of passion."[140]

149

A letter of May 21, 1944 was written on the occasion of the baptism of a friend's child. The context of the discussion was an air raid which Bonhoeffer hoped would not happen during a baptism. But, he said, "If in the middle of an air raid God sends forth the gospel summons into his Kingdom in Holy Baptism, that will be a clear sign of the nature and purpose of that Kingdom. For it is a Kingdom stronger than war and danger, a Kingdom of power and might, signifying to some eternal terror and judgment, to others eternal joy and righteousness, not a Kingdom of the heart, but one as wide as the earth, not transitory, but eternal, a Kingdom which makes a way for itself and summons men to itself to prepare its way, a Kingdom worthy of our life's devotion."[141]

In a July 21, 1944 letter Bonhoeffer meditated on the Christian and the world. He concluded that "it is only by living completely in this world that one learns to believe." For him, worldliness meant "taking life in one's stride, with all its duties and problems, its successes and failures, its experiences and helplessness. It is in such a life that we throw ourselves utterly in the arms of God and participate in his sufferings in the world and watch with Christ in Gethsemane. That is faith, that is *metanoia,* and that is what makes a man a Christian. How can success make us arrogant or failure lead us astray, when we participate in the sufferings of God by living in this world?" In the midst of his prison suffering Bonhoeffer could give thanks: "I am glad I have been able to learn it, and I know I could only have done so along the road I have travelled. So I am grateful and content with the past and the present. May God in his mercy lead us through these times. But above all may he lead us to himself!"[142]

Appended to an undated letter were a series of brief meditations Bonhoeffer called "Stations on the Road to Freedom." Here he wrote of the relationship of freedom to discipline, action, suffering and death. The only way one can be free, he believed, was through the discipline of both the senses and the soul. One must keep the body chaste and seek the goal set by God.

Only in doing a deed is there freedom, Bonhoeffer believed. He admonished, "Away with timidity and reluctance! Out into the storm of event, sustained only by the commandment of God and your faith, and freedom will receive your spirit with exultation." In this context he thought about how his free act in determining what he would do with his life had now brought suffering and bound his hands. "Yet," he said, "with a sigh of relief you resign your cause to a stronger hand, and are content to do so. For one brief moment you enjoyed the bliss of freedom, only to give it back to God that he might perfect it in glory."[143]

As late as August 10, 1944, in one of the last surviving letters from Bonhoeffer although he would not die for another eight months, he was still reflecting on prayer and taking it seriously. "It is just at such times as these that one should make a special point of thanksgiving in one's prayers. Above all, we should avoid getting absorbed in the present moment, and foster that peace of mind which springs from noble thoughts, measuring all things by them." He knew that God does not give people everything they want, but "he does fulfil his promises, i.e., he still remains Lord of the earth and still preserves his Church, constantly renewing our faith and not laying on us more than we can bear, gladening us with his nearness and help, hearing our prayers and leading us along the best and straightest road to himself. In this way God creates in us praise for himself."[144]

Eleven days later he made a strong reaffirmation of his own spirituality. "All that we rightly expect from God and pray for is to be found in Jesus Christ. The God of Jesus Christ has nothing to do with all that we, in our human way, think he can and ought to do. We must persevere in quiet meditation on the life, sayings, deeds, sufferings and death of Jesus in order to learn what God promises and what he fulfils. One thing is certain: we must always live close to the presence of God, for that is newness of life; and then nothing is impossible for all things are possible with God; no earthly power can touch us without his will, and danger can only drive us closer to him. We can claim nothing for ourselves, and yet we may pray for everything. Our joy is hidden in suffering, our life in death. But all through we are sustained in a wondrous fellowship. To all this God in Jesus has given his Yea and his Amen, and that is the firm ground on which we stand."[145]

Bonhoeffer spent the first eighteen months of his confinement in Tegel prison in Berlin where he was able to correspond rather freely. A July 20, 1944 attempt on Hitler's life failed and soon thereafter documents were discovered that related Bonhoeffer more clearly to the plot. In early October he was moved to the Gestapo prison in Prinz-Albert Strasse. This necessitated the destruction of many of Bonhoeffer's letters by his friends. Now Bonhoeffer's contacts were very restricted and the flow of letters was sharply reduced. In February 1945 he was moved to the death camp at Buchenwald. In early April he began to be moved to various places in Germany. While conducting a church service for his fellow prisoners in a schoolroom in Schöenberg, he was approached by two men who came with the fateful words, "Prisoner Bonhoeffer, get ready to come with us." All prisoners knew what that meant. He was taken to Flossenburg where, after a brief trial, he was hanged with other conspirators.

Payne Best, an English officer who was with Bonhoeffer in Schöenberg, reported that Bonhoeffer's last words to him were, "This is the end, for me the beginning of life." Then he asked Best to give a message to the bishop of Chichester in England.

Thus ended the life of one who maintained faith to the end under the most bitter and destructive circumstances. Perhaps that deep spiritual life is what sustained the courage of a Lutheran pastor so much admired today.

BIBLIOGRAPHY

Books by Dietrich Bonhoeffer:

Act and Being. New York: Harpers, 1956.
Christology. London: Collins, 1966.
Christ the Center. San Francisco: Harper and Row, 1978.
The Communion of Saints. New York: Harper and Row, 1963.
The Cost of Discipleship. Revised Edition. New York: Macmillan, 1963.
Creation and Fall. London: SCM Press, 1959.

Creation and Temptation. London: SCM Press, 1966.
Ethics. New York: Macmillan, 1955.
Life Together. New York: Harper and Row, 1954.
No Rusty Swords: Letters, Lectures and Notes 1928–1936. London: Collins, 1965.
Prayers from Prison. Philadelphia: Fortress Press, 1978.
Prisoner for God: Letters and Papers from Prison. New York: Macmillan, 1953.
Psalms: The Prayer Book of the Bible. Minneapolis: Augsburg, 1970.
Spiritual Care. Philadelphia: Fortress Press, 1985.
Temptation. New York: Macmillan, 1955.
True Patriotism: Letters, Lectures and Notes 1939–1945. New York: Harper and Row, 1973.
The Way to Freedom: Letters, Lectures and Notes 1935–1939. New York: Harper and Row, 1966.

Books about Dietrich Bonhoeffer:

Bethge, Eberhard, *Bonhoeffer: Exile and Martyr.* New York: Seabury, 1975.
Bethge, Eberhard, *Costly Grace.* San Francisco: Harper and Row, 1979.
Bethge, Eberhard, *Dietrich Bonhoeffer.* London: Collins, 1970.
Bosanquet, Mary, *The Life and Death of Dietrich Bonhoeffer.* London: Hodder and Stoughton, 1968.
Day, Thomas I., *Dietrich Bonhoeffer on Christian Community and Common Sense.* New York: E. Mellen Press, 1983.
Dumas, André, *Dietrich Bonhoeffer: Theologian of Reality.* New York: Macmillan, 1971.
Feil, Ernst, *The Theology of Dietrich Bonhoeffer.* Philadelphia: Fortress, 1985.
Goddard, Donald, *The Last Days of Dietrich Bonhoeffer.* New York: Harper and Row, 1976.
Godsey, John D., *The Theology of Dietrich Bonhoeffer.* Philadelphia: Westminster, 1960.
Gould, William Blair, *The Worldly Christian: Bonhoeffer on Discipleship.* Philadelphia: Fortress, 1967.

Kelly, Geffrey B., *Liberating Faith: Bonhoeffer's Message for Today*. Minneapolis: Augsburg, 1984.

Kuhns, William, *In Pursuit of Dietrich Bonhoeffer*. Dayton: Pflaum Press, 1967.

Marle, René, *Bonhoeffer: The Man and His Work*. New York: Newman Press, 1967.

Marty, Martin E., ed., *The Place of Bonhoeffer*. New York: Association Press, 1962.

Ott, Heinrich, *Reality and Faith: The Theological Legacy of Dietrich Bonhoeffer*. Philadelphia: Fortress, 1972.

Phillips, John A., *Christ for Us in the Theology of Dietrich Bonhoeffer*. New York: Harper and Row, 1967.

Phillips, John A., *The Form of Christ in the World: A Study of Bonhoeffer's Christology*. London: Collins, 1967.

Rasmussen, Larry L., *Dietrich Bonhoeffer: Reality and Resistance*. Nashville: Abingdon, 1972.

Roark, Dallas M., *Dietrich Bonhoeffer*. Waco, Texas: Word Books, 1972.

Smith, Ronald Gregor, *World Come of Age: A Symposium on Dietrich Bonhoeffer*. London: Collins, 1967.

Vorknik, Peter, *Bonhoeffer in a World Come of Age*. Philadelphia: Fortress, 1968.

Waelfel, James W., *Bonhoeffer's Theology: Classical and Revolutionary*. Nashville: Abingdon, 1970.

Zimmerman, Wolf Dieter, *I Knew Dietrich Bonhoeffer*. New York: Harper and Row, 1966.

CHAPTER VI

Dom Helder Camara

Dom Helder Camara has been one of the truly remarkable leaders of the third world in the twentieth century. A strong advocate for economic development and a critic of those political and economic structures that deliberately keep people in poverty, he is a fine example of a church leader who has combined an impressive social activism with a deep spirituality.

Born on February 7, 1909 in the *nordeste,* the northeastern part of Brazil, he rose steadily through ecclesiastical ranks to become the archbishop of Olinda and Recife. The son of a journalist and a primary school teacher in Fortaleza, Camara eventually enrolled in seminary and was ordained a priest in 1931. During the early 1930s he served as secretary for education in Ceara, his home state, and in 1936 he moved on to Rio de Janeiro where he was recognized as an expert in education, an interest that comes through in many of his books. Eventually he was appointed to the Supreme Council for Education in Brazil.

In 1952 he was named auxiliary bishop of Rio de Janerio. In that office he devoted himself to the problems of the *favelas,* the poverty stricken shanty towns found in Brazilian cities. In *The Conversion of a Bishop,* a dialogue with Camara, he explained his own personal evolution from an interest in "integrism," a form of Latin American fascism, to his concern about the exploitation of the poor through structures over which they had no control.

One of his passions was the organizing of Latin American

bishops in order to deal more effectively with Latin American problems of poverty and misery. For twelve years he served as the secretary general for the Conference of Brazilian Bishops and was instrumental in reorganizing the Latin American Episcopal Council (CELAM). A meeting of this council in Medellín, Colombia in 1968 was one of the milestones in the development of liberation theology.

Camara has been a disquieting presence in the Catholic Church. For example, in 1963 at the Second Vatican Council he urged the bishops to give up luxuries and privileges that alienated them from the working classes. He urged the abolition of titles such as "excellency" and "eminence," the renunciation of silver buckled shoes, limousines, rings with precious stones, gold and silver pectoral crosses and other symbols of wealth. In Recife he did not live in the episcopal palace, but in a small room in a church that had once served as the sacristy. He told the bishops, "Let us lose the mania of considering ourselves nobles and let us renounce our coats of arms and heraldic devices. Let us simplify our attire." He asked, "Have we or have we not adopted a capitalistic mentality, do we or do we not employ methods and proceedings quite suitable to bankers but not very suitable to a representative of Christ? Providence has already delivered us from the Papal States. When will the hour of God come which will bring the Church back to rejoin Lady Poverty?"[1]

Upon becoming archbishop of Olinda and Recife in April 1964, Camara addressed an introductory message to the people of the diocese. In his remarks he said, "Let no one be scandalised if I frequent those who are considered unworthy and sinful," and he reminded people that Christ said only the sick need a doctor. He added, "Let no one be alarmed if I am seen with compromising and dangerous people, of the left or the right, of establishment or opposition, with reformist and anti-reformist, revolutionary or anti-revolutionary, with those of good faith or bad." He did not want to be identified with any one group of people, but stated what would be the theme of his tenure, "My door and my heart will be open to everyone, absolutely everyone. Christ died for all men; I must exclude no one from fraternal dialogue."[2]

The new archbishop indicated to his diocese that his special love, like that of Christ, would be for the poor. "At the last judgment," he reminded, "we shall all be judged by our treatment of Christ, of Christ who hungers and thirsts, who is dirty, injured and oppressed." He distinguished between poverty and misery. Poverty may sometimes be accepted generously and offered as a gift to God, but misery is another matter. Misery, he said, "destroys the image of God which is in each of us; it violates the right and duty of human beings to strive for personal fulfilment."[3] Camara was convinced that Christ was present in the poor of his diocese. "Christ in the North-East is called Jose, Antonio, Severino. This is Christ, the name who needs justice, who has a right to justice, who deserves justice."[4]

The main goals of his work would be the reconstruction and development of his region. "Christ," he said, "gave to the hierarchy a mission which is specifically evangelical, but this does not mean that the Christian community must separate itself from the great adventure of progress."[5]

In articles in *Revolution Through Peace,* Camara developed a theology for economic development. "Our watchword for development," he said, "is the world of Christ: 'I came so that they may have life, and have it more abundantly.'"[6] Aware that many would accuse the church of abandoning heavenly truth for earthly reality, he sought to ground his development ideas on the love of God and the love of humankind, the two great commandments. We cannot love God, he said, without loving other people. "The struggle for economic development is Christian, profoundly Christian, as long as it is a synonym for brotherly love, for helping to rescue from misery millions of fellow creatures now existing in a subhuman state."[7]

The social revolution the world needs will not come by war. "It must be a profound and radical change requiring Divine Grace and a world movement to change public opinion, a movement which can and should be helped and encouraged by the Church."[8] God gave humans the right and the duty to have dominion over nature and complete the work of creation. The problem with violent change is that it happens so quickly there is no time for inner change to develop. Camara concluded, "It is useless to dream of reforming the socioeconomic structure, the outer structure, of our lives as long as there is not a correspondingly deep change in our inner selves."[9]

Christians committed to social justice in Brazil have often suffered persecution. In 1968, for example, Camara's episcopal residence was machine-gunned, and there are many stories of tortured and murdered priests. An anonymous Brazilian priest reported in the December 7, 1973 issue of *Commonweal* that Camara on more than one occasion presented himself to the military police with bag packed, offering to exchange himself for those arrested. The government has attempted to diminish his influence by barring any news of him from press, radio, or television.

SPIRITUALITY AND SOCIAL ACTION

Dom Helder Camara is an example of a Christian who attempted to combine a deep spirituality with social action. In a book *Charismatic Renewal and Social Action: A Dialogue* by Camara and Cardinal Leon-Joseph Suenens, he was described by the cardinal as "the bishop of the poor who is speaking of our social duties, but it is also the bishop who spends many hours of the night in prayer and is ever conscious of the link between God's ascendancy and his own action."[10] Later, in a chapter of his own, Camara said that the gifts of the Holy Spirit are of value only if they are placed at the service of human love. Speaking to charismatics, he said, "He who has no love and humility cannot advance on the Lord's path, not even by one step. I invite you all to live under the action of the Spirit and, at the same time, to let yourselves be led by him to the very heart of the world, to the heart of men's problems. You have to pray and act at one and the same time." Evangelization and humanization "go hand in hand."[11]

Prayer was a fundamental part of Camara's life. It puts us, he said, into direct contact with God. "Without prayer, there is no current, no Christian respiration."[12] He described how, after his ordination, he realized that he would have to devote regular time and space to prayer, speaking and listening to God. Otherwise, he would find himself depleted with nothing to offer either the Lord or other people. He felt blessed that God had given him the ability to wake up and go to sleep at will, enabling him to arise at two o'clock every morning to pray for two hours.

His first concern upon waking up in the middle of the night was to restore a sense of unity within himself, a unity which is in Christ. Oneness with Christ produces oneness with others, "for when Christ and I are one, how delightful it is to speak to our Father in the name of all men, of all times and all places."[13]

His prayer also included the regular praying of the breviary as well as eucharistic prayer. "The Eucharist," he said, "envelops the whole day in wonder, because everything, in all simplicity, becomes Offertory, Consecration, Communion."[14]

Camara also stressed the importance of communal prayer. True community celebrations of prayer, he believed, relived the days of early Christianity when the ideal was to be "one heart and one soul in Christ."[15]

The archbishop gave some warnings to charismatics. They should never use prayer as a pretext for neglecting social action. In drawing strength from renewal in the Spirit, the movement should help the church to overcome its "triumphalist temptations" and be a living presence of Christ in the service of others. People should see the union of prayer and commitment and understand that the cross has both vertical and horizontal arms.

CONVERSION

Camara spoke frequently of his own conversion from an establishment Latin American clergyman to a bishop concerned about the poor and the powerless. He said that as a seminary student and young priest he suffered from "the general blindness." A concern for authority and order had prevented him from facing the realities of injustice. He preached that suffering should be accepted in union with Christ, and, in doing so, became simply a tool of the authorities.[16] "We had been so blinded then by the need to maintain, sustain and support authority and social order that we couldn't see the terrible, cruel injustices that this authority and social order permitted. But as soon as we began to realize the truth and face up to it, we had to think and act in a different way."[17]

It was difficult for Camara not to be judgmental toward the reactions of the rich. He admitted that if he had been born into a wealthy family and never had any encounters with human misery, his reactions would be just like those of the rich that opposed him. But he raised the question, "How dare we look at Christ if we who wear his name as our shield and call ourselves his disciples are contributing, for our part, to the scandal of the century: a small minority enjoying vast means of existence and enrichment while the great majority of God's sons are reduced to a subhuman condition?"[18]

What was it that opened the eyes of his generation? "On the one hand," he said, "the reality that appeared more and more brutal." The other influence was Pope John XXIII, "who reinforced our faith in the active presence of the Holy Spirit."[19]

A good part of Camara's career, 1931–1948, was spent in the field of education. This included positions as director of the Department of Education in the state of Ceara, as technical advisor to the Ministry of Education in Rio de Janeiro and as a member of the Higher Council of Education. Most secondary and higher education took place in Catholic schools, and Camara later lamented that opportunities to educate the sons of the rich on social problems had not been taken. There had been a need to awaken the human spirit, expand the human heart, and overcome selfishness. Gradually, he began to see the requirements of a true education.

In *The Conversion of a Bishop,* the interviewer asked Dom Helder Camara if he had changed his understanding of religion over the years. His reply was negative. The gospel is so rich and people can see only certain aspects of it. It has not changed, he said. "It is I who, by the grace of the Lord, and with the help of my friends, my brothers, have had the opportunity of seeing certain aspects of my religion that I did not see at first. Christ is mysterious to us."[20]

However, for Camara conversion was not a one time event; it was a continuing process. He told of visiting a convent to celebrate the sixtieth year of profession of one of the nuns. When he asked the woman how many years she had been in religious life, she answered, "Honestly, Father, I've spent one day in the religious life. Because every day I have to start all over again." He regarded that as a remarkable answer. "We are never completely converted," he said. "We have to keep on converting ourselves every day."[21] In facing the social problems of the world Camara said, "Without a deep personal conversion, no one can become an instrument for the conversion of the world."[22]

VOCATION

Reflecting on his own priestly vocation, Camara recalled an incident from his childhood. His parents did not practice their religion very regularly, but one day his father spoke to Camara about his desire to become a priest. "My boy, priest and self-centeredness don't go together. A priest isn't his own master. He has only one reason for living: to live for others." Camara said that this statement reflected what the Lord had already sown in his heart. "All my life I've lived the dream of being one with Christ to help my fellow-beings conquer their self-centeredness."[23]

When someone raised the question of priestly celibacy, Camara said that even if it were optional for priests, he would still choose the celibate life because of the freedom it gave him. If he had family responsibilities, he would be more restricted in what he could do in his ministry.

A major part of the archbishop's conversion was a strong identification with the poor, a conversion he urged upon others. He did not call for neglect for one's immediate family, but did admonish, "Refuse to be locked within the narrow circle of your immediate family. Decide to take on the whole family of mankind." He also urged, "Make the sufferings and humiliations of all your brothers your own. Live on a global scale, or better still take the whole universe."[24]

Camara told of an incident in the mid 1960s where he visited a sugar plantation in Recife. At a given time, all of the workers, who lived in subhuman conditions, gathered around the landowner and his family to hear the archbishop speak. After a mass the workers returned to their houses and Camara shared a lavish meal with the landowner. He shocked his host, however, by saying that he did not want to sleep in the great house, but with one of the poor families. He wanted to experience their poverty. "I wanted to experience for myself, to give myself a jolt," he said. The landowner finally persuaded him to sleep in the chapel, which he did. But Camara knew that the chapel belonged to the landowner and was there to help the workers accept their fate. Religion was being used as the opium of the people.[25]

Poverty was Camara's great concern. While he worried about nuclear war, he saw poverty as an even greater problem. "War is daily becoming more absurd," he wrote. "It is literally true that it could be the collective suicide of mankind. But as well as nuclear warfare and biological warfare we also have poverty, the most bloody, evil and shameful war of them all."[26]

The great scandal of the twentieth century, Camara believed, was that two-thirds of the people in the world lived in subhuman conditions, suffering from hunger and wretchedness. People know how to eliminate that kind of suffering. The scientific and technological knowledge exists to do it. But such an accomplishment would conflict with the values of the arms race, with the "wasteful characteristics of a consumer society," with national security as a supreme value, and with the goals of multinational corporations.[27] However, he believed that "the egoism of the rich presents a more serious problem than Communism," and that the real threat to the peace of the world is "the atom bomb of squalid poverty."[28]

Camara speculated on the parable of the rich man and Lazarus. Suppose the man of wealth had invited Lazarus to his table. Lazarus would probably have been ashamed to come because of his poverty, his dirty clothes and body. How could he have felt comfortable talking to a man of wealth? So the poor are reduced to coming to the rich as beggars.

If the poor themselves took up arms against the rich they would be destroyed. Their only hope would be if a superpower would help them, and then the superpower would try to control the situation. The possibility of the rich north inviting the poor south to a dialogue was like the rich man inviting Lazarus. Real conversation would be impossible. When such dialogue occurs now, the south is always represented by the wealthy elite. The poor of the southern hemisphere will have to unite before there can be any significant north-south dialogue.

THE CHURCH

Camara described the church as "the continuation of Christ's life on earth." The greatest temptation confronting the church was the temptation of power. Although it is divine in that Christ founded it, it is at the mercy of human weakness, specifically the weaknesses of its leaders. "But," he said, "even at the mercy of our weakness, the Church still belongs to Christ. The Spirit of God watches over it." Still, today it is tempted by money and profit and will have to reform itself. "The Spirit of God," he believed, "will tear the Church of Christ free of the trammels of money. 'Tear' is the word. It will emerge bleeding and naked, more beautiful than ever."[29] If it is to be the presence of Christ in the world, the church must "cast off its concern for prestige . . . unharness itself from the chariot of the mighty, and . . . agree to live the prophecy of the Master, 'Behold, I send you out as sheep in the midst of wolves.' " The poverty which God asks of the church now is "to sever all compromises with governments and the powerful, and to commit itself to the service of the poor, the oppressed, the destitute, who are made to live subhuman lives."[30]

One of the main functions of the church, Camara believed, was to be prophetic, to proclaim the word of God, and "to lend the Lord's voice to those who have no voice."[31] In *Revolution Through Peace,* he wrote, "It would be an unpardonable scandal if the Church were to abandon the masses in their hour of greatest need, as if she took no interest in helping them reach a level of human, Christian dignity compatible with real citizenship."[32]

Although devoted to it, Camara was not above criticizing the church. He knew that for many years it had been used to support the establishment in Brazil. He reported an occasion where he was the speaker at a university in a diocese where the bishop, a young man, was very conservative. During a question period following the lecture a young woman criticized the bishop and asked Camara if he knew what the man was like.

Camara responded to the young woman that while the church was a divine institution, it suffered from human failings. He then proceeded to list a number of the human failings of the papacy, the curia, the nuncios and those of bishops and priests. But he also mentioned the human failings of the laity and called for collaboration rather than confrontation between laity and hierarchy. Both sides should recognize the reality of human failings and try to enter into dialogue, which, he knew, was very difficult. "We are all novices in the art of dialogue," Camara said. "Truth is so vast that each of us can see only one angle, one aspect of it. If only we could piece our little glimpses together, instead of fighting one another."[33]

The temptation many dedicated people faced was to leave the church because of its resistance to progress. Camara insisted, however, that such people must try to reform and revitalize the church from within. They should not feel alone. There are many who have the same ideals. However, reformers always run the risk of being misunderstood, and there is the danger that they will be punished for their efforts. But, said Camara, "This is excellent training for attacking and overcoming socio-economic and political-cultural structures. You will be able to take the measure of your courage, prudence, loyalty, kindness, power of decision and responsibility." However, Camara was convinced that it is impossible to live or work effectively without some kind of structure and organization. "Unfortunately even those structures which are most effective and reasonable to begin with always become intolerable after a while."[34] But people in every field are frustrated by structures that inhibit their work. There are minorities everywhere ready to unite for reform, and that is a source of hope.

Camara wrote a little poem which included these lines:

> Only when we—
> the church and each of us—
> are not attached to privileges, power, and money,

can we serve you fully.
Let us pour out our lives
in the service of our neighbor!
That is the best way
of serving you and observing
the one and only commandment:
love of God and humankind.[35]

Camara's view of the papacy was to see the pope as a pastor. He knew that the sovereignty of the Vatican State was necessary to maintain the independence of the pope, but this made it impossible for popes to travel as pastors. They were always treated as heads of state. He felt that recent popes such as John XXIII and Paul VI suffered from "the errors of the past." He knew they would rather be pastors than heads of state and rejoiced when such men performed little acts such as opening doors for themselves or removing their coats unassisted to show that they were ordinary human beings like Peter and Paul.

In the past Camara believed that the Brazilian church had achieved an ideal balance between church and state. But now, he said, "I am calmly convinced that the Church's only engagement and solidarity should be with the people. If the government too becomes engaged with the people, then a fruitful meeting between Government and Church can take place at this level."[36]

Camara criticized the Inquisition of past centuries while speaking of modern political regimes that use torture. "If you compare the instruments of torture used today with those used by the Inquisition, there isn't very much difference," he said. "It's impossible to understand how man can have remained so primitive." He added, "What can we do to wake people up and make them realize what's happening?"[37]

The archbishop lamented, "As a Christian, a Catholic and a churchman, I am devoted to my Mother, the Church. And it's because I love her that I am so demanding. I don't like it when she disillusions people, and disappoints them, particularly young people. And I wonder how much longer she is going to keep arriving too late."[38]

Camara did have ecumenical interests. He remarked once that

if Luther had found himself with a John XXIII the scandal of schism might have been avoided. He praised the pope for working for ecumenism. "Efforts are being made everywhere now to reconcile our differences," he noted. Remembering that in the past Catholics were not allowed to read Protestant Bibles, he was pleased that "Today we have the same books, the same texts and, very often, especially when times are bad, we pray and work together."[39]

The archbishop was not uncritical about church life. He raised serious questions. "Are we so alienated that we can worship God at our ease in luxurious temples which are often empty in spite of all their liturgical pomp, and fail to see, hear and serve God where he is present and where he requires our presence, among mankind, the poor, the oppressed, the victims of injustices in which we ourselves are often involved?"[40]

THE HOLY SPIRIT

A belief in the presence and work of the Holy Spirit was fundamental in Camara's spirituality. He felt that the value of the charismatic movement today was its continual reminding that the Holy Spirit is a present reality. It is seen most clearly in human life. He told a story of a woman who was about to be evicted from her house. The police took her to the landlord before whom she was terrified. But she called on the Holy Spirit who enabled her to confront the man successfully. "That's how we know the Holy Spirit is here, present, alive," he said. "Never tell me it's hard to visualize the Holy Spirit. The Holy Spirit is our contemporary, living with us, helping us. What could our weakness do in moments of crisis, were it not for the strength of the Spirit of God."[41]

He told a similar story about a woman named Annonciade who lived in a *favela,* a shanty town, in northeastern Brazil. The woman could neither read nor write. When an effort was made to evict the residents and destroy the *favela,* this woman tried to organize the community to resist peacefully. She was picked up by the police and taken in for interrogation. Fearful of what might happen, that she might betray God and her friends, she remembered the words of

Christ, "When you are brought before the tribunal, don't worry about the answers you are to give. The Spirit of the Lord will speak in your stead." The authorities could have caused her disappearance or tortured her to death, but strangely she was released because of the answers she gave to the questions. Camara said, "She gave answers so powerful and so beautiful that later on she could not repeat them."[42]

Camara spoke of the changes in the ways that priests are trained. In the past, candidates for the priesthood would be isolated from the people for many years. Today, he says, young candidates want to be among the people, for this is where the Holy Spirit is at work. "If something changes in a particular place in a specific town, district or village, you may think it's the result of an idea, or the actions, of an individual or group, or a current fashion. But when it's the same idea and attitude that springs up at more or less the same time, here, there, and everywhere—all over—then you know it's the breath of the Holy Spirit."[43]

Pope John XXIII was credited by Camara with reinforcing "our faith in the active presence of the Holy Spirit!" The pope announced that the Holy Spirit had inspired him to summon an ecumenical council because the reform of the church was the preliminary step to Christian unity.[44]

Camara had a great sense of the universality of the work of the Holy Spirit. He felt that he and the people of Recife were trying hard to obey the promptings of the Holy Spirit. But, he said, "You know the Holy Spirit doesn't have to wait for missionaries and bishops to transmit its message; it doesn't stop to choose the places where there are Catholics. They are everywhere, potentially: all men are the sons of God, united through Christ. So the Holy Spirit breathes; and very often when the missionaries arrive they are really surprised to find that the Holy Spirit has got there first."[45]

One of the functions of the Holy Spirit that Camara saw at work was in the presence of minority opinions at episcopal conferences. In such minorities, said Camara, "it is the Holy Spirit who evokes the ideas and who does the work." He added, "We have to understand what the Holy Spirit tells us through the Gospel and through the entire history of the Church up to the last Council. We need a minority in the Vatican that can understand and enact not only episcopal collegiality, but also co-responsibility in the Church of the Lord; that can understand and enact the primacy of the Pope in terms of service and love . . . not as a kind of super-state, but as an instrument to serve all of God's people."[46]

In speaking about various non-violent and peace groups throughout the world, Camara said, "The Holy Spirit has inspired all of these different groups throughout the world and only the Holy Spirit can make them effective."[47]

REVOLUTION

In a conversation with Cardinal Montini, the future Pople Paul VI, Camara expressed concern about Vatican censorship. It had gotten a bit out of hand and Camara said, "I'm quite sure that certain passages in the Gospel could be censored. For instance, the Magnificat is a revolutionary hymn: it's disturbing, it's serious, it's agitation! It speaks out against the established order, against the rich and powerful! It may not be Communism, but it prepared the way for Communism. No doubt someone will underline it in red ink!"[48]

Camara felt it was impossible to be neutral. It you were not on the side of the oppressed, you were supporters of the oppressors. It was important, however, that in advocating for the oppressed they do not seek the only kind of advancement they have ever seen, to become the new oppressors. Nothing is gained by transforming the oppressed into the oppressors.

Young people, noted Camara, were particularly impatient when the church produced encyclicals and other great documents advocating social justice and the church has been slow in implementing them. "Fortunately, young people reject all this false prudence," he said, "which I'm sure Christ Himself is the first to reject. But it's a human weakness of the Everlasting Church."[49]

Camara was concerned that some young people in their desire to defeat injustice were ready to use violence. But, he felt, violent means will only call down violent repression. Still, he was moved by the courage of the young who were imprisoned and tortured. People would not endure that just for materialist ideas.

Although accused of being a communist, Camara condemned communism. "If we condemn the serious failures of the capitalist super-states like the US and EEC," he wrote, "we must likewise condemn the communist super-states, the USSR and China."[50] But, he said, communist infiltration is not the danger. Communism will become a danger for us only if people do not attack the structures of slavery and call anyone demanding social justice a communist. "Let us not forget," he said, "that while people are dying in the name of communism or anti-communism, the capitalist and communist empires are perfectly able to agree when their interests demand it."[51] The real threat to peace is injustice. "When will governments and the privileged understand that there can be no true peace until justice has been established?"[52]

He was concerned that some church officials saw Marxism in some of the youth movements that advocated liberation theology. He reminded people that the 1968 conference in Medellín, Colombia, made up of bishops representing all the episcopal conferences of Latin America, was as official as it could possibly be. It had been called by the pope, opened by him at the end of a eucharistic conference in Bogota, and three personal representatives of the pope had remained for the meeting. Every resolution passed had been approved by Rome, even those calling for the changing of social structures to overcome institutionalized injustice.

The negative reaction from the privileged classes was inevitable. They were so loyal to the church that they could not criticize it directly, but they had to assume that the problem was Marxist infiltration among the students and the clergy. Camara knew why some youth groups had become so radical. "The crime these young people committed was to believe that the decisions of the Second Vatican Council were not meant to remain on paper."[53]

For Camara, revolution did not mean violence and armed combat. Rather, "it means the radical and swift change of unjust structures. It has nothing to do with the numerous revolutions Latin America has seen already, which have often resulted in a change of personnel, but never in a change of structures."[54]

169

NONVIOLENCE

Camara was convinced that liberation "could never be achieved through armed struggle." In conversation with young people who thought violence might be the only solution to the problems of the poor, Camara tried to discourage them by raising a number of questions. Suppose they were able to rob a bank successfully without killing anyone and had some money. Where would they buy arms? And if they could buy them, "How effective are these weapons going to be against the enormous supplies of armaments that the Pentagon supplies to our governments, which form a major part of the supposed aid to under-developed countries. My friends, there is no point in taking up arms against the forces who manufacture arms and wars." Those countries that were liberated by violence soon found themselves under the control of new masters. Latin America has had two hundred and fifty years of political independence without economic independence. "The forces that need poor countries, and need poor countries to stay poor, are very skillful at exploiting the weaknesses of people who are ill-prepared for liberty. That is always the aftermath of victory."[55]

Camara greatly admired Martin Luther King, Jr. He said, "I have always seen, and I still see, the Negro movement in the United States as an outstanding example of active nonviolence." He was particularly interested in this because he believed that "the battle against racial discrimination in the United States was only one aspect of the struggle to liberate the Third World."[56]

He also felt that terrorism was counterproductive. "I have never been able to understand, much less sympathize with, methods like the taking of hostages. As far as I am concerned, the end can never justify the means." Terrorism only gives governments the opportunity to increase repression under the guise of protecting the people.[57]

He was, however, unhappy with the term "nonviolence." He did not like anything that communicated the idea of passivism, and preferred a term like "the violence of pacifists." Young people could not be expected to renounce violence unless they saw some other approach that could achieve concrete results.[58]

The real key to social change, Camara believed, was education. In Rio de Janerio he was appointed as a technical adviser in education. He felt at the time that there was a "blindness to the real requirements of a Christian education. Oh, if only we'd been able to understand and interpret religious events, and the living presence of Christ, to communicate to children, and young people, and adults, rich and poor alike, the terrific strength that can come from true religion." Even within the bourgeois structures, he said, there were people who were hungry for true Christianity.[59]

In 1947 Camara was appointed the deputy padre-general of Catholic Action for all of Brazil. One of his first moves was to set up a secretariat for Catholic Action. This made possible the organizing of regional meetings of bishops to explore the problems of the people and the development of special branches of Catholic Action. The primary accomplishment was "opening people's eyes to human problems." Catholic Action went right into the midst of workers, peasants, students and other groups. Naturally this aroused the opposition of the privileged classes who, upon being found out, began to accuse the church of changing religion and turning people against the rich.

CAPITALISM

Camara had a number of opinions about the role of capitalism in Brazil. When the church began seriously to investigate social problems, he said, it became clear that the major problem was not a conflict between capitalism and communism or east and west. Rather, it was a matter of capitalism exploiting the east-west conflict and presenting itself as the savior of civilization. In reality, he said, the roots of capitalism are entirely materialistic. "We wanted people to realize that within our own country and continent there is the scandal of internal colonialism; and that on an international level there is the scandal of rich countries who maintain their wealth by keeping poor countries in misery." Camara insisted, "Our main concern was to make sure that the people would no longer be exploited." One of the major problems, he admitted, was the church. "We were aware that we ourselves had manipulated the people; we had used them to defend a certain kind of morality. We had been so blinded then by the need to maintain, sustain and support authority and social order that we couldn't see the terrible, cruel injustices that this authority and social order permitted."[60]

The hunger and misery of the third world was the result of unjust structures and injustice. Camara said bluntly, "The Lord demands of us that we denounce the injustices. This is part of proclaiming the Word. Denunciation of injustice is an absolutely essential chapter in the proclamation of the Gospel."[61]

Multinational corporations, said Camara, came to the third world with the promise of new jobs, technology and a stable currency. In reality, however, there was economic growth only for the few. For people as a whole there was more foreign debt and few new jobs because technology reduced the need for workers. The workers that were required needed technical training too advanced for the "nonwhite indigenes." The result was the destruction of native cultures and a practical enslavement. The present hope, however, is that unlike the past the church is now denouncing injustice.

The archbishop was very blunt: "There is no hope of our people being liberated through Capitalism." The problem is with a system that puts profit over a concern for people. The multinational company, which Camara called "the most advanced element of Capitalism," only makes the poor poorer and the privileged richer.[62] There could be no political independence without economic independence, he believed.

In the little book *Through the Gospel with Dom Helder Camara,* the archbishop commented on the story of Jesus cleansing the temple in John 2:13–16. He noted that people today are concerned about vendors of candles, medals, and statuettes that are found near large churches in South America. That, however, is not a serious problem, compared to other problems created by Christians. He mentioned the Christian countries of Europe and North America that become wealthier by exploiting the poor of other countries. "And the Christian part of the Third World—Latin America—is now copying the very injustices committed by the wealthy Christian countries. I should think Christ may well consider taking the whip to us from time to time."[63]

And, he believed, the capitalistic democracies could not survive without war industries. He mentioned an incident at Vatican II where a declaration was being prepared that totally condemned war. A delegation of North American workers, however, opposed that condemnation, saying that the result would be economic collapse and unemployment. Camara advocated the setting up of a peace college which could study the problem of how to develop an economy without dependence upon war industries.

The problem for the third world was not a lack of resources, Camara believed. It was human selfishness. "There's enough land for everyone, there's enough food for everyone. But as long as we put profit before humanity, we shall always end up in these same idiotic situations: overproduction here, under-nourishment there." He was amazed that in an age of computers and space travel, the human race could not solve these problems. "We're still no better than monkeys," he said. "We're unable to overcome our own selfishness."[64]

GOD

Dom Helder Camara had a strong naturalistic element in his theology. People tended to find God in creation, he believed. Although people do not see God personally, God's presence and power "remain beyond doubt" for him. It is in God that "we breathe and act and find our being," for God wants to draw people "into the very intimacy of his own life."[65]

For Camara, God was not distant. He affirmed the presence of God, especially at particular times, such as times of temptation. He especially recognized the power of sexual temptations, but, he said, "the presence of God is very much stronger. We have God on our side."[66]

However, Camara did not believe that faith was simple. In commenting on the story of the Canaanite woman who was rejected by Jesus until her imaginative reply about dogs eating the crumbs from the table (Matthew 15:21–28), he confessed that he often argued with God: "I know you want to test our faith. I know you. But you know our weakness even better. Don't give this impression of being distant, remote, of not listening. I know you're here, quite close, attentive, listening to everything. So why give the wrong impression?"[67]

Camara was convinced that God was not unjust although there may be the appearance of that. God does not "refuse anyone the indispensable." However, some people are given unusual gifts and more is demanded of them. "He asks more from those to whom he gives more. They are not greater or better, they have greater responsibility. They must give more service. Live to serve." In fact, God drives some people to "take a leap in the dark," and these may be called upon to bear witness in some hour of trial. But, God will support and encourage them.[68]

How does one know God or hear God? Camara was a man of prayer and that was one living link with the divine. But he also felt that the voice of God was speaking through the poor. "The protests of the poor are the voice of God," as are the voices of countries suffering injustices. "It is not difficult to hear God's call today in the world about us," Camara believed, but it is difficult to offer an adequate response and be converted.[69] Still, he said, God "is far less likely to abandon us in hardship than in times of ease."[70]

Anyone who believed that God is the Father of all people was, by virtue of that belief, "committed to ties of human brotherhood and solidarity."[71] Likewise, God lives in human communities and hears the cries of the people in them.

The ultimate hope for the resolving of human problems, for Camara, was God. He wrote a brief poem on the subject.

> Hope without risk
> is not hope,
> which is believing
> in risky loving,
> trusting others
> in the dark,

174

the blind leap
letting God take over.[72]

His poetic advice was:

Go down
into the plans of God.
Go down
deep as you may.
Fear not your fragility
under the weight of water.
Fear not
for life or limb
sharks attack savagely.
Fear not the power
of treacherous currents under the sea.
Simply, do not be afraid.
Let go. You will be led
like a child whose mother
holds him to her bosom
and against all comers is his shelter.[73]

Camara ended his little book *Hoping Against All Hope* with a long prayer. Near the end he said:

Lord, you may think the ending of this prayer
somewhat naive—
There is but one richness:
participating in your life, your divinity,
your creative power, your will.[74]

CHRIST

Camara affirmed a strong faith in Christ. "I am as sure of Christ's existence as I am of my own hand with its five fingers. I can touch and see. I meet Jesus every day. And we are one. No doubt about it."[75]

Theologically, Camara believed that Christ was God made

human. This same God revealed in Christ desires us to become children by adoption in Jesus Christ. (Charismatic, 14–15) This same Christ has "restored the divine resemblance tainted from the time of the first sin." In Christ human nature has been raised to an "unparalleled dignity."[76] God has been united with every person through Christ the redeemer. One implication of this is that Christians who are giving themselves to working in subhuman situations are recognized by the light of Christ radiating in them.

He had the same outlook Dorothy Day expressed about seeing Christ in the poor. "I am absolutely certain Christ is present under the weakness of the poor," said Camara.[77] He was aware that because of their hopelessness the poor often seek refuge in drunkenness. People often told the bishop that he could not possibly see Christ present in these idle drunkards who do not want to work. In such situations, Camara admitted, the poor become "like things, objects, animals. They lose their self-respect. But when I look at them from close up, I recognize the face of Christ in them."[78] Elsewhere Camara reminded that Christ said that "whoever is suffering, humiliated, crushed is he. In our own times when more than two-thirds of the human race are living in sub-human conditions, it's easy enough to meet him in the flesh."[79] Camara said that he could not specify a time when he became aware of the presence of Christ in those who suffer. Christ probably was not recognizable on the cross, either, after his suffering. But the bishop spoke of that other eucharist, "the Eucharist of the Poor, under the appearance of misery. The Real Presence in the poor."[80]

During his night vigils, Camara talked with Christ. He said that at these times he tried to recover his unity with Christ by going over with him the events and encounters of the day. But he also affirmed a constant, unclouded awareness of Christ.

In fact, Camara believed that Christ was present with people who have never heard of him. "Christ is everywhere," he said, "with God's entire creation, and not merely with those who know him. The only difference between Christians who do know Christ and the others who don't is that we have greater responsibilities."[81]

Camara had a tremendous sense of the incarnation. He saw no

need to visit Bethlehem at Christmas, when Christ is born every moment of the day. For example, he mentioned how large corporations would buy up land, and families that had lived there for years would have to leave. They would go to the cities, such as Recife, and put together a miserable hovel, a sub-hovel. The wife would often be pregnant and there Christ would be born.

Camara believed that by baptism all share in Christ's holiness. But holiness for him was not having visions or performing miracles. "It means living by sanctifying grace, constantly mindful that we carry Christ within us and that we walk within God."[82] And, he believed, what a great thing it would be if people looking at us would not see us but Christ in us. "Ah, how perfect that would be!"[83] "We churchmen," he said, "ought to be Christ's living presence among his people."[84]

"We must imitate Christ. Christ came for everybody, for all people of all countries and all times. But nevertheless He became incarnate in one race, in one society. He adopted a language and customs that were not the languages and customs of all people of all countries and all times. He was the son of a Nazareth carpenter. We need to understand this lesson of incarnation; we must each remain bound to humanity as a whole, and to the universal Church, but at the same time become incarnate in our own particular Nazareth."[85]

Camara gave a new facet to the image of Christ as the good shepherd. "Do you know what sheep it is that Christ bears on His shoulders as He walks today's roads? All you have to do is open your eyes and look around you: the Good Shepherd is carrying on His shoulders the underdeveloped world."[86]

The first lines of *Hoping Against Hope* are:

> Put your ear to the ground
> and listen,
> hurried, worried footsteps,
> bitterness, rebellion.
> Hope
> hasn't yet begun.
> Listen again.

Put out feelers.
The Lord is there.
He is far less likely
to abandon us
in hardship
than in times of ease.[87]

THE MASS

The presence of Christ in the mass was essential in Camara's faith, for it made possible a very intimate relationship with the Lord. He once wrote, "Whenever I say mass, I can almost hear the Father looking at me and saying, 'This is my beloved Son.' "[88] "It is wonderful," he said, "when distributing the Eucharist, to be absolutely certain I'm handing out not pieces of bread but the living Christ. This gives me immense joy."[89] He spoke of how he felt a need to protect Christ from the wind and weather when the Lord is present in the ciborium or on the paten. This was a sign of how Christ makes himself weak in the world.

Camara spoke of a sense of overwhelming awe that he felt about the mass. He said that he was amazed that priests could survive it, "seeing the Son of God come down into our hands, having him there before our eyes, actually holding him. How can we support this immense weight?"[90]

Taking communion at mass was more than just receiving Christ. Camara believed that it was assuming the infinite dimensions of Christ's heart, of embracing the whole human race with the love of Christ.

CAMARA'S FAITH

Camara was convinced that the essence of faith is invisible. It is a matter of discovering the hidden dimension of things. We can easily describe externals without mentioning what is most important, the presence of God everywhere. Likewise, "The Lord makes big things out of little ones. Without humility you might look down from the height of perfection and simply not understand, or begin to imagine, the miracles that Christ performs with human weakness."[91]

The grace of God often comes to people in surprising ways. Dom Helder told of a decisive moment of grace in his life that occurred in connection with a eucharistic congress he had organized in Brazil. At the end of the congress Cardinal Gerlier of Lyons, France praised Camara's organizing ability which, he believed, made the congress such a success. He challenged Camara to use that talent in the service of the poor. Camara regarded that statement as a sign of grace, a major turning point in his life. "The grace of the Lord came to me through the presence of Cardinal Gerlier. Not just through the words he spoke: behind his words was the presence of a whole life, a whole conviction. And I was moved by the grace of the Lord. I was thrown to the ground like Saul on the road to Damascus."[92] Although he had been aware of the poverty of the people, now he felt that the Lord had opened his eyes to the reality of the poor and he dedicated his life and ministry to them.

However, Camara believed that the call to serve was not based on merit. "When the Lord fixes his choice, this isn't to reward merit, nor is it to confer an honour. It's to call that person to serve more strenuously than others, in his name."[93]

The Virgin Mary is a major element in the piety of Brazilian Catholics. The great national sanctuary is at Aparecida, and there are many stories of the Virgin appearing there. People go there on pilgrimages throughout the year. Camara told a story of this piety being used to oppose a proposed law allowing divorce. Cardinal Leme, who opposed the idea, took the statue of Our Lady of Aparecide throughout the country, and it was greeted by enormous crowds, a testimony to the people's devotion to the church and, by implication, opposition to the divorce law.[94]

But what of the popular beliefs about Mary? Camara conceded that in some places devotion to Mary may be stronger than to Christ, but, he said, "Christ, and Christ alone, is our redeemer." Still, he felt that simple Marian piety had much to commend it. People who ridiculed it, he said, often would not leave their houses until they knew if the day was lucky for business or love. Others lived by superstitions, such as refusing to go on the thirteenth floor of a building. "How silly!" he said. "I prefer my own people's simplicity."[95]

He believed that apparitions of Mary were possible. "Why shouldn't she appear to bring comfort, encouragement and help? Why not?"[96] Marian piety, he believed, was no more absurd than some of the popular eastern cults that attracted young people.

Camara affirmed, "Mary lived all the great mysteries of God. What a part she played in the incarnation! What a part she played in the redemption! What a part she plays today in the Church! Believe me, we can feel Mary's presence, she is present in every moment of crisis; as a mother, she is always with us, watching over us."[97]

In Brazilian Catholicism, Mary was often confused with Iemanja, the goddess of the sea. Camara said that when he saw great crowds gather to celebrate the immaculate conception, he was convinced that two-thirds of the people were probably thinking of Iemanja. This represented a mixture of African religion and Christianity. He did not worry too much about that, however. He said that names were unimportant. People often confuse his name. "It's the same with the Mother of God, who is also the Mother of Men, and the Mother of Fishermen: it really doesn't matter if people confuse Her name with that of Iemanja!"[98]

One of his interests in Mary, obviously, was her identification with the poor. In a prayer to Mary he expressed the desire

> to sing with you
> that Magnificat that exalts the poor,
> with no bitterness,
> but with such fullness of love
> that if this song wounds anyone,
> it leaves only a benign wound
> with its own power to heal.[99]

Another significant element in Camara's piety was his belief in angels. He said that all the arguments of theologians could never change his simple devotion to a guardian angel. He called this angel

José and affirmed, "I can't possibly doubt him: I should be not only ungrateful, but blind, if I did."[100] José helped him through many difficult situations. He told of an incident when he had an audience with Monsignor Montini, a future pope. He woke up that morning with an ear infection, unable to hear. But José helped him get through the audience successfully, able to hear everything.

Camara's writings were grounded in optimism based on his faith. One of his themes was, "Let us keep hoping! We can change our lives, transform our hearts!" (Hope, 10)

He talked about hope in the midst of suffering. It is easy for people in good health to talk about the value of suffering, but it is another matter for those who suffer. Yet Camara told stories about suffering people who had not lost hope. A friend who worked with the poor in a sacrificial way became paralyzed on one side. The man's response was, "I have begun to move out; half is already gone." Another friend, a woman, had half of her face eaten away by cancer. She asked the archbishop to offer mass in her room so she might unite her suffering with that of Christ.[101] (Hope, 20–21)

One of the great sources of hope for Camara was the young. Their idealism to create a more just and humane world was a constant inspiration to him. The non-violent Pax Christi International was one example. He took comfort in the fact that all over the world there were "many extraordinary young people, full of hope and generosity, ready to give all that they value most to build a better world."[102] He was also encouraged by scientists who, having brought wretchedness to much of the human race, are now concerned with safeguarding humanity. And he was encouraged by the fact that the religions of the world are drawing closer together and helping create justice and love in the world.

SIN AND EVIL

Sin and evil are realities that manifest themselves in a variety of ways. Among the major threats to interior peace, said Camara, are bitterness, harshness and sadness. These feelings weaken us and make our problems worse.

Temptation, however, is unavoidable. It is not important not to be tempted. What is important is not to give in to temptation. But, he felt, there are good temptations, "calls to walk in faith, in love of God and God's creation. They are calls to get up again and walk in hope."[103]

The chief cause of injustice in the world, Camara believed, was selfishness. He had hopes that the new scientific knowledge that the earth is a speck of dust among the stars would make humankind more modest and humble and create a sense of solidarity with the rest of the human race. This was a sign of hope that humanity would be liberated from selfishness.

The place to begin dealing with selfishness was the self. "Self-ishness must be resisted actively and intelligently first of all within each one of us."[104]

Even in the realm of spirituality there were temptations. In his "prayer for the rich" he said,

> There is a dangerous and degenerate kind of wealth:
> to be proud
> of one's humility, poverty, and mortifications,
> of one's mystical communion.[105]

One of the obvious characteristics of Camara's life was his personal humility. He believed that humility made it possible for one to laugh at oneself without bitterness when failure occurred. The humble person is not surprised or astonished at failure, but is ready to begin anew without wasting any time.

ATHEISTS AND NON-CHRISTIANS

Camara had some remarkable things to say about atheists and non-Christians. He felt that in religions all over the world there were people ready to sacrifice for a more just and humane world. He urged non-Christians, "Translate into your own language the truths I speak which are not the creations of personal fantasy but realities experienced together by all those who belong to the same spiritual family."[106] He made the same statement to atheistic humanists. "Translate what I say in my language into your language. When I talk of God, translate, perhaps by 'nature', 'evolution', what you will." He concluded, "Accept our friendship. We will learn to understand each other and we will be able to go forward together."[107]

Camara believed that atheists and Christians should try to understand each other better. Belief in God does not necessarily enslave anyone. In educating people for freedom the help of atheists would be needed, and Christians should understand that atheistic humanists could show a genuine love for humankind. After all, he said, "Anyone who loves his neighbor is already fulfilling half the law."[108]

Camara suggested that Catholic universities should work at establishing a dialogue with atheists. The fact is, he said, that atheism almost always arises from weaknesses in the lives and thoughts of believers. He specifically mentioned three atheists who represented what was most lofty and worthy of respect and love. The three were the evolutionist Julian Huxley, the psychoanalyst Erich Fromm, and the Marxist Roger Garaudy. Evolutionists must see that Christians have lost their fear of the concept and that a belief in a Creator gives some meaning to evolution. Psychoanalysts need to reexamine the idea that religion is neurosis. Marxists need to see that the church is working for a better society and world.

Many young people had turned to atheism, Camara believed, because they were disappointed in believers who did not practice what they preached. On the other hand, some atheists were examples to believers by their courage in facing suffering and torture for the sake of justice and peace. For Camara, anyone "who lives the truth, and has the courage to work for peace in this way, will see God."[109]

On the religious level, he believed, "Religions are uniting to show that love of men is a special way of loving God. They are trying to preach the gospel to the poor who have been made subhuman by their living conditions, so that they may know the truth which will help them get rid of their poverty, and to the rich, who have become inhuman through their excesses, so that they may know the truth which will help them become human again."[110] Camara suggested a congress in which each religion would describe the truths in its tradition which would help humanize the world.

Dom Helder Camara, with great personal courage, has been a prophetic voice calling the world to repentance. Sensing the crucifixion taking place again in the unjust suffering of people, he has refused to compromise with those powers that would use religion to justify or mask the pain of oppression. He has seen Christ in the midst of human misery, and his personal piety was centered on a deep relationship with his Lord. He lived a moderately ascetic life, rejecting the privileges of position and power, and has sought to identify with those to whom Christ seemed to give major attention, the poor and suffering of the world.

BIBLIOGRAPHY

Books by Dom Helder Camara:

Charismatic Renewal and Social Action: A Dialogue. With Cardinal Léon-Joseph Suenens. Ann Arbor: Servant Books, 1979.

The Church and Colonialism. Denville, New Jersey: Dimension Books, 1969.

The Conversions of a Bishop. With José de Broucher. Glasgow: Collins, 1979.

The Desert Is Fertile. Maryknoll, New York: Orbis Books, 1974.

Hoping Against All Hope. Maryknoll, New York: Orbis Books, 1984.

It's Midnight, Lord. Washington, D.C.: The Pastoral Press, 1984.

Race Against Time. Denville, New Jersey: Dimension Books, 1971.

Revolution Through Peace. New York: Harper and Row, 1971.

Spiral of Violence. London: Sheed and War, 1971.

A Thousand Reasons for Living. Philadelphia: Fortress Press, 1981.

Through the Gospel with Dom Helder Camara. Maryknoll, New York: Orbis Books, 1986.

Books about Dom Helder Camara:

Broucker, José de, *Dom Helder Camara: The Violence of a Peacemaker.*
Maryknoll, New York: Orbis, 1960.

Cheetham, Neville, *Helder Camara.* People with a Purpose Series 3.
London: SCM, 1973.

Hall, Mary, *The Impossible Dream: The Spirituality of Dom Helder
Camara.* Maryknoll, New York: Orbis Books, 1980.

Hall, Mary, *A Quest for the Liberated Christian.* Las Vegas: Lang,
1978.

Kent, Bruce, *The Non-Violence of Helder Camara.* London: Catholic
Truth Society, n.d.

Conclusion

What can be concluded from the study of these six people? All were concerned about social issues, though they may have emphasized different areas. Martin Luther King, Jr. sought racial justice. Dag Hammarskjöld worked for world peace. Dietrich Bonhoeffer sought to live the gospel under the threat of the Nazi regime and believed that Hitler had to be destroyed or western civilization would be in peril. Simone Weil was concerned about unemployment and the devastating effect of the modern industrial machine on the individual. Dorothy Day and Dom Helder Camara found the presence of Christ in the poor and searched for alternative economic systems.

There were many commonalities. Martin Luther King, Jr. was often quoted in Dorothy Day's *Catholic Worker*. Camara was also interested in King. Hammarskjöld and Weil were both mystics who wrote in their journals about their experiences. Both saw mystical insights as important keys to peace and the resolution of social problems.

King saw a moral force at work in the universe moving humanity toward justice, while Bonhoeffer, in the context of Bible reading and prayer in a Gestapo prison cell, wondered how people could be religious after Nazism. Weil sought to experience poverty and the lot of the worker in order to understand better the human condition when she easily could have chosen a life of relative ease and comfort. Hammarskjöld managed to keep his deep religious life to himself so that his friends were surprised to discover this side of him. They had never known those deep feelings and experiences that motivated him. Dom Helder Camara made the pilgrimage from supporting facism for the sake of public order to an heroic and daring witness for the rights of the poor.

Even in death these people were remarkable. King and Bonhoeffer were modern Christian martyrs. Weil starved herself to death rather than seek privileges unavailable to many others. Hammarskjöld's death may have been accidental, but there is some evidence that it might have been a murder. Camara's life has been constantly threatened and his episcopal residence has been machine gunned on occasion. Only Dorothy Day had what might be called a normal, natural death, but to the end she remained firm in her commitment to the witness of poverty.

King changed the character of American society and, along with Camara, showed the possibilities of nonviolence. Day, Weil, and Camara would not let the world forget the plight of the poor, of those who suffer because of conditions they cannot control. Bonhoeffer showed the world how to live the gospel under the most difficult circumstances, and Hammarskjöld demonstrated the possibility of living the mystical life while devoting one's life to politics and government.

What did religious experience contribute to their social activism? That is a question to be pondered deeply. Perhaps it gave them a greater sensitivity to human problems. Surely it gave them courage to live heroically. It did not make them perfect, and all have their detractors. They lived high risk lives. King, Camara, and Bonhoeffer were often threatened with death. Weil and Day deliberately chose poverty and insecurity. Although surely someone would have provided for them, they never asked for that. Hammarskjöld's work at the United Nations sometimes put him in high risk situations such as that in which he died.

It would be unfair to call any of these people ideologues, although all had deep ideological commitments. They had confidence in their knowledge of what God wants for people, namely justice, peace, and the necessities of life.

Books on King, Weil, and Day continue to appear with frequency. Bonhoeffer is still a standard part of the curriculum of any quality theological school. Camara is studied as part of the growing interest in the third world. *Markings* remains in print and will probably be seen in the future as one of the great spiritual classics of the twentieth century.

The relationship between religion and social action is worthy of much study. It was faith that led King, Hammarskjöld, and Bonhoeffer to action. A concern for the poor and suffering of the world led Day and Weil to faith and Camara to a new understanding of faith and church. So the process seems to work in both directions.

The basic point of this study has been to show that there is no necessary conflict between deep personal religious experience and social action. Each feeds and nourishes the other. These six people are examples of a well-balanced religious life: a commitment to social justice and a deep personal spiritual life. If this study has caused the reader to ponder this reality, it has accomplished its purpose.

Notes

INTRODUCTION

1. Claude Geffre and Gustavo Gutierrez, eds., *The Mystical and Political Dimensions of the Christian Faith* (New York: Herder and Herder, 1974), p. 28.

Chapter I: MARTIN LUTHER KING, JR.

1. Martin Luther King, Jr., *Stride Toward Freedom* (New York: Harper and Brothers, 1958), pp. 69–70.
2. *Stride Toward Freedom,* p. 92.
3. Martin Luther King, Jr., *Strength to Love* (New York: Harper and Row, 1963), p. 109.
4. *Stride Toward Freedom,* pp. 106–107.
5. *Stride Toward Freedom,* p. 25.
6. Martin Luther King, Jr., *The Trumpet of Conscience* (New York: Harper and Row, 1967), p. 75.
7. *Strength to Love,* p. 110.
8. *Strength to Love,* p. 115.
9. Martin Luther King, Jr., *Why We Can't Wait* (New York: Harper and Row, 1963), p. 97.
10. *Stride Toward Freedom,* p. 224.
11. *Stride Toward Freedom,* p. 224.
12. *Stride Toward Freedom,* p. 59.
13. *Stride Toward Freedom,* p. 63.
14. *Stride Toward Freedom,* p. 117.

15. *Stride Toward Freedom*, pp. 134–136.
16. *Why We Can't Wait*, p. 75.
17. *Stride Toward Freedom*, p. 169.
18. *Strength to Love*, pp. 131–132.
19. *Strength to Love*, p. 23.
20. *Strength to Love*, p. 124.
21. *Strength to Love*, p. 144.
22. *Strength to Love*, p. 109.
23. *Strength to Love*, p. 107.
24. *Strength to Love*, p. 83.
25. *Strength to Love*, p. 83.
26. *Strength to Love*, p. 92.
27. *Strength to Love*, p. 91.
28. *Strength to Love*, p. 84.
29. *Strength to Love*, p. 83.
30. *Strength to Love*, p. 109.
31. *Strength to Love*, p. 15.
32. *Strength to Love*, p. 16.
33. *Strength to Love*, p. 95.
34. *Strength to Love*, p. 135.
35. *Strength to Love*, p. 136.
36. *Strength to Love*, pp. 133–134.
37. *Strength to Love*, p. 65.
38. *Strength to Love*, p. 65.
39. *Strength to Love*, p. 65.
40. *Strength to Love*, p. 11.
41. *Strength to Love*, pp. 44–45.
42. *Strength to Love*, p. 147.
43. *Strength to Love*, p. 148.
44. *Stride Toward Freedom*, p. 91.
45. *Stride Toward Freedom*, p. 97.
46. *Stride Toward Freedom*, p. 139.
47. *Strength to Love*, p. 148.
48. *Strength to Love*, p. 149.
49. *Stride Toward Freedom*, p. 100.
50. *Stride Toward Freedom*, pp. 96–97.
51. *Stride Toward Freedom*, p. 15.
52. *Stride Toward Freedom*, p. 103.
53. *Stride Toward Freedom*, pp. 98–99.
54. *Stride Toward Freedom*, p. 99.

55. *Stride Toward Freedom*, p. 101.
56. *Stride Toward Freedom*, p. 84.
57. *Stride Toward Freedom*, p. 85.
58. *Stride Toward Freedom*, p. 87.
59. *Stride Toward Freedom*, pp. 102–107.
60. *Why We Can't Wait*, pp. 24–25.
61. *Why We Can't Wait*, p. 28.
62. *Why We Can't Wait*, p. 34.
63. *Why We Can't Wait*, p. 61.
64. *Why We Can't Wait*, p. 79.
65. *Why We Can't Wait*, pp. 79–81.
66. *Why We Can't Wait*, p. 88.
67. *Why We Can't Wait*, p. 91.
68. Martin Luther King, Jr., *Where Do We Go From Here: Chaos or Community?* (New York: Harper and Row, 1967), p. 45.
69. *Where Do We Go From Here*, p. 46.
70. *Where Do We Go From Here*, p. 49.
71. *Where Do We Go From Here*, p. 50.
72. *Where Do We Go From Here*, p. 57.
73. *Where Do We Go From Here*, pp. 57–58.
74. *Where Do We Go From Here*, p. 61.
75. *Where Do We Go From Here*, pp. 63, 66.
76. *Strength to Love*, p. 64.
77. *Why We Can't Wait*, p. 61.
78. *Stride Toward Freedom*, p. 205.
79. *Trumpet of Conscience*, p. 72.
80. *Why We Can't Wait*, p. 92.
81. *Strength to Love*, p. 18.
82. *Stride Toward Freedom*, p. 25.
83. *Why We Can't Wait*, pp. 94–95.
84. *Why We Can't Wait*, p. 96.
85. *Why We Can't Wait*, pp. 96–97.
86. *Why We Can't Wait*, p. 135.
87. *Where Do We Go From Here*, p. 75.
88. *Where Do We Go From Here*, p. 96.
89. *Where Do We Go From Here*, p. 99.
90. *Where Do We Go From Here*, p. 100.
91. *Why We Can't Wait*, p. 95.
92. *Strength to Love*, p. 21.
93. *Strength to Love*, p. 63.

94. *Strength to Love,* p. 63.
95. "I Have a Dream," in James Melvin Washington, *Testament of Hope* (San Francisco: Harper and Row, 1986), pp. 219–220.

Chapter II: SIMONE WEIL

1. Simone Weil, *The Need for Roots* (New York: Putnam's, 1952), pp. v–vi.
2. George A. Panichas, *The Simone Weil Reader* (New York: David McKay, 1977), pp. xvii–xviii.
3. Mark Gibbard, *Twentieth Century Men of Prayer* (London: SCM Press, 1974) p. 25.
4. Simone Weil, *Waiting for God* (New York: Putnam's, 1951), p. 15.
5. *Waiting for God,* p. 18.
6. Gibbard, p. 26.
7. Simone Weil, "Factory Journal," *Formative Writings 1929–1941* (Amherst: University of Massachusetts Press, 1987), p. 160.
8. "Factory Journal," p. 171.
9. "Factory Journal," p. 225.
10. Simone Petrement, *Simone Weil: A Life* (New York: Pantheon Books, 1976), p. 245.
11. *Waiting for God,* pp. 66–67.
12. *Waiting for God,* p. 67.
13. *Waiting for God,* pp. 67–68.
14. *Waiting for God,* p. 68.
15. *Waiting for God,* p. 69.
16. Simone Weil, *Gravity and Grace* (New York: Putnam's, 1952), p. 5.
17. *Gravity and Grace,* p. 16.
18. *Gravity and Grace,* pp. 16–17.
19. *Gravity and Grace,* p. 32.
20. *Gravity and Grace,* p. 45.
21. *Gravity and Grace,* p. 45.
22. *Gravity and Grace,* p. 47.
23. *Gravity and Grace,* p. 48.
24. *Gravity and Grace,* p. 48.
25. *Gravity and Grace,* p. 49.
26. *Gravity and Grace,* p. 50.
27. *Gravity and Grace,* pp. 53–54.
28. *Gravity and Grace,* p. 111.

29. *Gravity and Grace*, pp. 163–164.
30. *Waiting for God*, p. 69.
31. *Waiting for God*, p. 69.
32. *Waiting for God*, p. 71.
33. *Waiting for God*, p. 72.
34. *Waiting for God*, p. 72.
35. *Waiting for God*, p. 88.
36. *Waiting for God*, p. 62.
37. *Waiting for God*, p. 62.
38. *Gravity and Grace*, p. 162.
39. *Gravity and Grace*, p. 112.
40. *Gravity and Grace*, p. 168.
41. *Waiting for God*, p. 89.
42. *Waiting for God*, p. 90.
43. *Gravity and Grace*, p. 167.
44. *Gravity and Grace*, p. 85.
45. *Gravity and Grace*, pp. 78–79.
46. *Gravity and Grace*, p. 115.
47. *Gravity and Grace*, p. 61.
48. *Gravity and Grace*, p. 115.
49. *Gravity and Grace*, p. 84.
50. *Gravity and Grace*, pp. 141–142.
51. *Gravity and Grace*, p. 111.
52. *Gravity and Grace*, p. 114.
53. *Gravity and Grace*, p. 143.
54. *Gravity and Grace*, p. 89.
55. *Waiting for God*, p. 133.
56. *Waiting for God*, pp. 133–134.
57. *Waiting for God*, pp. 44–45.
58. *Waiting for God*, p. 83.
59. *Gravity and Grace*, p. 139.
60. *Waiting for God*, p. 89.
61. *Waiting for God*, pp. 117–118.
62. *Waiting for God*, pp. 119–120.
63. *Waiting for God*, p. 121.
64. *Waiting for God*, p. 123.
65. *Waiting for God*, p. 123.
66. *Waiting for God*, pp. 124–125.
67. *Waiting for God*, p. 125.
68. *Waiting for God*, pp. 131–132.

69. *Waiting for God,* p. 132.
70. *Waiting for God,* pp. 135–136.
71. *Gravity and Grace,* p. 57.
72. *Waiting for God,* p. 72.
73. *Gravity and Grace,* p. 82.
74. *Gravity and Grace,* pp. 142–144.
75. *Gravity and Grace,* p. 166.
76. *Waiting for God,* pp. 49–50.
77. *Waiting for God,* pp. 62–63.
78. *Waiting for God,* p. 65.
79. *Waiting for God,* p. 74.
80. *Waiting for God,* p. 54.
81. *Waiting for God,* pp. 75–76.
82. *Waiting for God,* p. 70.
83. *Waiting for God,* pp. 77–78.

Chapter III: DAG HAMMARSKJÖLD

1. Henry P. Van Dusen, *Dag Hammarskjöld: The Statesman and His Faith* (New York: Harper and Row, 1964), p. 4.
2. Sven Stolpe, *Dag Hammarskjöld: A Spiritual Portrait* (New York: Scribners, 1966), p. 19.
3. Van Dusen, p. 22.
4. Stolpe, p. 30.
5. Stolpe, p. 38.
6. Stolpe, p. 31.
7. Aulen, pp. 10–11.
8. Van Dusen, pp. 46–47.
9. Van Dusen, p. 106.
10. Aulen, p. 51.
11. Van Dusen, p. 131.
12. Stolpe, p. 33.
13. Dag Hammarskjöld, *Markings* (New York: Knopf, 1978), p. 103.
14. Van Dusen, p. 192.
15. Van Dusen, pp. 144–145.
16. Van Dusen, p. 145.
17. Van Dusen, p. 145.
18. *Markings,* p. 144.
19. *Markings,* p. 5.
20. *Markings,* p. 8.

21. *Markings,* p. 55.
22. *Markings,* p. 66.
23. *Markings,* p. 67.
24. *Markings,* p. 79.
25. *Markings,* p. 89.
26. *Markings,* p. 127.
27. *Markings,* p. 133.
28. *Markings,* p. 143.
29. *Markings,* p. 150.
30. *Markings,* p. 164.
31. *Markings,* p. 189.
32. *Markings,* p. 12.
33. *Markings,* p. 13.
34. *Markings,* p. 90.
35. *Markings,* p. 92.
36. *Markings,* p. 100.
37. *Markings,* p. 101.
38. *Markings,* p. 104.
39. *Markings,* p. 105.
40. *Markings,* p. 108.
41. *Markings,* p. 110.
42. *Markings,* p. 110.
43. *Markings,* p. 117.
44. *Markings,* p. 149.
45. *Markings,* p. 156.
46. *Markings,* p. 8.
47. *Markings,* p. 83.
48. *Markings,* p. 97.
49. *Markings,* p. 127.
50. *Markings,* p. 205.
51. *Markings,* pp. 214–215.
52. *Markings,* p. 122.
53. *Markings,* p. 57.
54. *Markings,* p. 16.
55. *Markings,* p. 58.
56. *Markings,* p. 16.
57. *Markings,* p. 81.
58. *Markings,* p. 76.
59. *Markings,* p. 76.
60. *Markings,* p. 76.

61. *Markings,* p. 82.
62. *Markings,* p. 165.
63. *Markings,* p. 40.
64. *Markings,* p. 77.
65. *Markings,* p. 71.
66. *Markings,* p. 96.
67. *Markings,* p. 117.
68. *Markings,* p. 16.
69. *Markings,* p. 84.
70. *Markings,* p. 92.
71. *Markings,* p. 97.
72. *Markings,* p. 145.
73. *Markings,* p. 151.
74. *Markings,* p. 91.
75. *Markings,* p. 120.
76. *Markings,* p. 205.
77. *Markings,* p. 205.
78. *Markings,* p. 9.
79. *Markings,* p. 69.
80. *Markings,* p. 157.
81. *Markings,* p. 199.
82. *Markings,* p. 194.
83. *Markings,* p. 78.
84. *Markings,* p. 53.
85. *Markings,* p. 97.
86. *Markings,* p. 19.
87. *Markings,* p. 191.
88. *Markings,* p. 154.
89. *Markings,* p. 117.
90. *Markings,* p. 121.
91. *Markings,* p. 43.
92. *Markings,* p. 47.
93. *Markings,* p. 149.
94. *Markings,* p. 63.
95. *Markings,* p. 43.
96. *Markings,* p. 150.
97. *Markings,* p. 156.
98. *Markings,* p. 83.
99. *Markings,* p. 140.
100. *Markings,* p. 104.

101. *Markings,* p. 194.
102. *Markings,* p. 93.
103. *Markings,* p. 43.
104. *Markings,* pp. 24–25.
105. *Markings,* p. 90.
106. *Markings,* p. 78.
107. *Markings,* p. 95.
108. *Markings,* p. 104.
109. *Markings,* p. 64.
110. *Markings,* p. 109.
111. *Markings,* p. 101.
112. *Markings,* p. 104.
113. *Markings,* p. 104.
114. *Markings,* p. 15.
115. *Markings,* p. 158.
116. *Markings,* p. 89.
117. *Markings,* p. 166.
118. *Markings,* p. 14.
119. *Markings,* p. 82.
120. *Markings,* p. 67.
121. *Markings,* p. 48.
122. *Markings,* p. 53.
123. *Markings,* p. 48.
124. *Markings,* p. 42.
125. *Markings,* p. 150.
126. *Markings,* p. 122.
127. *Markings,* p. 77.
128. *Markings,* p. 147.
129. *Markings,* p. 133.
130. *Markings,* p. 6.
131. *Markings,* p. 61.
132. *Markings,* p. 87.
133. *Markings,* p. 85.
134. *Markings,* p. 13.
135. *Markings,* p. 159.
136. *Markings,* p. 46.
137. *Markings,* p. 44.
138. *Markings,* p. 82.
139. *Markings,* p. 80.
140. *Markings,* p. 159.

141. *Markings,* p. 73.
142. *Markings,* p. 106.
143. *Markings,* p. 82.

Chapter IV: DOROTHY DAY

1. William D. Miller, "Dorothy Day," *Saints Are Now,* ed. by John J. Delaney (Garden City, NY: Doubleday, 1983), p. 19. Miller is the author of the two major biographies of Dorothy Day: *A Harsh and Dreadful Love* (New York: Liveright, 1973) and *Dorothy Day: A Biography* (San Francisco: Harper and Row, 1982).
2. Cesar Chavez, "Always There," *Catholic Worker,* December 1980, p. 7.
3. Daniel Berrigan, *Portraits of Those I Love* (New York: Crossroad, 1982), p. 72.
4. Nancy L. Roberts, *Dorothy Day and the Catholic Worker* (Albany: State University of New York Press, 1984), p. 21.
5. Dorothy Day, *The Long Loneliness* (San Francisco: Harper and Row, 1952), p. 78.
6. *The Long Loneliness,* p. 81.
7. *The Long Loneliness,* p. 84.
8. *Dorothy Day and the Catholic Worker,* p. 23.
9. *The Long Loneliness,* p. 105.
10. *The Long Loneliness,* p. 139.
11. *Dorothy Day and the Catholic Worker,* p. 33.
12. *Dorothy Day and the Catholic Worker,* p. 35.
13. *Dorothy Day and the Catholic Worker,* pp. 37–38.
14. *The Catholic Worker,* May 1965, p. 3.
15. *The Catholic Worker,* June 1979, p. 2.
16. *The Catholic Worker,* November 1960, p. 3.
17. *The Catholic Worker,* July–August 1962, p. 1.
18. *The Catholic Worker,* June 1963, p. 3.
19. *The Catholic Worker,* May 1970, p. 2.
20. *The Catholic Worker,* May 1970, p. 2.
21. *The Catholic Worker,* January 1980, p. 6.
22. *The Catholic Worker,* June 1970, pp. 1–2.
23. *The Catholic Worker,* May 1973, p. 8.
24. *The Catholic Worker,* January 1980, pp. 1, 6.
25. *The Catholic Worker,* January 1980, p. 1.
26. *The Catholic Worker,* February 1971, p. 8.

27. *The Catholic Worker,* March–April 1976, p. 2.
28. *The Catholic Worker,* September 1976, p. 1.
29. *The Catholic Worker,* July–August 1976, p. 2.
30. *The Catholic Worker,* July–August 1976, p. 6.
31. *The Catholic Worker,* May 1978, p. 8.
32. *The Catholic Worker,* December 1980, p. 7.
33. *The Catholic Worker,* March 1981, p. 3.
34. *The Catholic Worker,* December 1980, p. 7.
35. *The Catholic Worker,* December 1980, p. 8.
36. *The Catholic Worker,* July–August 1960, p. 7.
37. *The Catholic Worker,* July–August 1960, p. 7.
38. *The Catholic Worker,* March–April 1973, p. 6.
39. *The Catholic Worker,* July–August 1973, p. 2.
40. *The Catholic Worker,* June 1976, p. 2.
41. *The Catholic Worker,* July–August 1974, p. 2.
42. *The Catholic Worker,* November 1961, p. 2.
43. *The Catholic Worker,* October–November 1972, p. 4.
44. *The Catholic Worker,* October–November 1972, p. 2.
45. *The Catholic Worker,* February 1980, p. 7.
46. *The Catholic Worker,* June 1973, p. 2.
47. *The Catholic Worker,* July–August 1975, p. 2.
48. *The Catholic Worker,* December 1969, p. 5.
49. *The Catholic Worker,* December 1969, p. 5.
50. *The Catholic Worker,* October–November 1975, p. 8.
51. *The Catholic Worker,* October–November 1975, p. 8.
52. *The Catholic Worker,* July–August 1978, p. 2.
53. *The Catholic Worker,* January 1962, p. 1.
54. *The Catholic Worker,* September 1962, p. 2.
55. *The Catholic Worker,* March 1966, p. 6.
56. *The Catholic Worker,* March 1966, p. 8.
57. *The Catholic Worker,* December 1962, p. 2.
58. *The Catholic Worker,* September 1962, p. 2.
59. *The Catholic Worker,* March 1966, p. 6.
60. *The Catholic Worker,* March 1966, p. 6.
61. *The Catholic Worker,* October 1968, p. 5.
62. *The Catholic Worker,* September 1976, p. 5.
63. *The Catholic Worker,* June 1961, pp. 2, 6.
64. *The Catholic Worker,* June 1960, p. 2.
65. *The Catholic Worker,* September 1962, p. 6.
66. *The Catholic Worker,* January 1965, p. 8.

67. *The Catholic Worker,* March 1966, p. 8.
68. *The Catholic Worker,* September 1965, p. 6.
69. *The Catholic Worker,* September 1966, p. 2.
70. *The Catholic Worker,* January 1967, p. 1.
71. *The Catholic Worker,* September 1962, p. 1.
72. *The Catholic Worker,* May 1970, p. 11.
73. *The Catholic Worker,* May 1970, p. 11.
74. *The Catholic Worker,* May 1970, p. 11.
75. *The Catholic Worker,* September 1965, p. 6.
76. *The Catholic Worker,* February 1969, p. 2.
77. *The Catholic Worker,* January 1970, p. 2.
78. *The Catholic Worker,* December 1976, p. 2.
79. *The Catholic Worker,* July–August 1965, p. 4.
80. William D. Miller, *Dorothy Day: A Biography* (San Francisco: Harper and Row, 1982), p. 517.

Chapter V: DIETRICH BONHOEFFER

1. Eberhard Bethge, *Costly Grace* (New York: Harper and Row, 1979), p. 13.
2. Bethge, *Costly Grace,* p. 26.
3. Bethge, *Costly Grace,* p. 38.
4. *Act and Being* (New York: Harpers, 1956), p. 170.
5. *Act and Being,* p. 177.
6. *No Rusty Swords* (London: Collins, 1965), p. 66.
7. *No Rusty Swords,* p. 75.
8. *No Rusty Swords,* p. 79.
9. *No Rusty Swords,* pp. 82–87.
10. *No Rusty Swords,* p. 116.
11. *No Rusty Swords,* p. 119.
12. Bethge, *Costly Grace,* p. 46.
13. Bethge, *Costly Grace,* p. 47.
14. Bethge, *Costly Grace,* p. 49.
15. Bethge, *Costly Grace,* p. 56.
16. Bethge, *Costly Grace,* p. 57.
17. Eberhard Bethge, *Dietrich Bonhoeffer* (New York: Harper and Row, 1979), p. 194.
18. Bethge, *Dietrich Bonhoeffer,* p. 61.
19. Bethge, *Costly Grace,* p. 228.
20. *No Rusty Swords,* pp. 219, 221.

21. *No Rusty Swords,* p. 225.
22. *No Rusty Swords,* pp. 237–238.
23. *No Rusty Swords,* pp. 244–245.
24. *No Rusty Swords,* p. 230.
25. *No Rusty Swords,* p. 233.
26. *No Rusty Swords,* p. 69.
27. Bethge, *Costly Grace,* p. 75.
28. Bethge, *Costly Grace,* p. 77.
29. *The Cost of Discipleship* (New York: Macmillan, 1963), p. 45.
30. *The Cost of Discipleship,* p. 46.
31. *The Cost of Discipleship,* p. 37.
32. *The Cost of Discipleship,* p. 37.
33. *The Cost of Discipleship,* p. 40.
34. *The Cost of Discipleship,* p. 41.
35. *The Cost of Discipleship,* p. 49.
36. *The Cost of Discipleship,* p. 50.
37. *The Cost of Discipleship,* p. 52.
38. *The Cost of Discipleship,* p. 55.
39. *The Cost of Discipleship,* p. 58.
40. *The Cost of Discipleship,* p. 58.
41. *The Cost of Discipleship,* p. 60.
42. *The Cost of Discipleship,* pp. 63–64.
43. *The Cost of Discipleship,* pp. 69–70.
44. *The Cost of Discipleship,* p. 76.
45. *The Cost of Discipleship,* p. 93.
46. *The Cost of Discipleship,* p. 93.
47. *The Cost of Discipleship,* p. 94.
48. *The Cost of Discipleship,* p. 97.
49. *The Cost of Discipleship,* p. 98.
50. *The Cost of Discipleship,* p. 99.
51. *The Cost of Discipleship,* p. 99.
52. *The Cost of Discipleship,* p. 100.
53. *The Cost of Discipleship,* p. 105.
54. *The Cost of Discipleship,* p. 100.
55. *The Cost of Discipleship,* p. 101.
56. *The Cost of Discipleship,* p. 181.
57. *The Cost of Discipleship,* p. 181.
58. *The Cost of Discipleship,* p. 181.
59. *The Cost of Discipleship,* p. 183.
60. *The Cost of Discipleship,* p. 189.

61. *The Cost of Discipleship*, p. 190.
62. *The Cost of Discipleship*, pp. 190–191.
63. *The Cost of Discipleship*, p. 194.
64. *The Cost of Discipleship*, p. 196.
65. *The Cost of Discipleship*, p. 267.
66. *The Cost of Discipleship*, p. 281.
67. *The Cost of Discipleship*, p. 301.
68. *The Cost of Discipleship*, p. 312.
69. *The Cost of Discipleship*, pp. 313–314.
70. *The Cost of Discipleship*, p. 337.
71. *The Cost of Discipleship*, p. 341.
72. *The Cost of Discipleship*, p. 343.
73. *The Cost of Discipleship*, p. 343.
74. *Life Together* (New York: Harper and Row, 1954), p. 17.
75. *Life Together*, p. 20.
76. *Life Together*, p. 25.
77. *Life Together*, p. 27.
78. *Life Together*, p. 42.
79. *Life Together*, p. 51.
80. *Life Together*, p. 54.
81. *Life Together*, p. 71.
82. *Life Together*, pp. 72–73.
83. *Life Together*, p. 73.
84. *Life Together*, pp. 73–74.
85. *Life Together*, p. 79.
86. *Life Together*, p. 80.
87. *Life Together*, p. 81.
88. *Life Together*, p. 82.
89. *Life Together*, p. 84.
90. *Life Together*, pp. 83–84.
91. *Life Together*, pp. 84–85.
92. *Life Together*, p. 85.
93. *Life Together*, p. 99.
94. *Life Together*, pp. 85–86.
95. *Life Together*, p. 87.
96. *Life Together*, p. 88.
97. *Life Together*, p. 99.
98. *Life Together*, p. 47.
99. *Life Together*, p. 45.
100. *Life Together*, p. 46.

101. *Life Together,* p. 47.

102. *Psalms: The Prayer Book of the Bible* (Minneapolis: Augsburg, 1970), pp. 10–11.

103. *Psalms,* p. 11.

104. *Psalms,* pp. 20–21.

105. *Psalms,* p. 26.

106. Bethge, *Costly Grace,* p. 84.

107. Bethge, *Dietrich Bonhoeffer,* pp. 626–627.

108. Bethge, *Dietrich Bonhoeffer,* p. 627.

109. *The Way to Freedom* (New York: Harper and Row, 1966), p. 228.

110. *The Way to Freedom,* p. 228.

111. *The Way to Freedom,* pp. 228–229.

112. *The Way to Freedom,* pp. 230–231.

113. *The Way to Freedom,* pp. 232–233.

114. *The Way to Freedom,* p. 233.

115. *The Way to Freedom,* pp. 234–235.

116. *The Way to Freedom,* p. 241.

117. *The Way to Freedom,* pp. 241–242.

118. *The Way to Freedom,* pp. 238–239.

119. *The Way to Freedom,* p. 241.

120. *The Way to Freedom,* p. 246.

121. *The Way to Freedom,* p. 247.

122. See G.K.A. Bell, "The Background of the Hitler Plot," *Contemporary Review,* October 1945.

123. *Prisoner for God: Letters and Papers from Prison* (New York: Macmillan, 1953), p. 36.

124. *Prisoner for God,* pp. 35–37.

125. *Prisoner for God,* pp. 37–38.

126. *Prisoner for God,* pp. 41–42.

127. *Prisoner for God,* p. 54.

128. *Prisoner for God,* p. 71.

129. *Prisoner for God,* p. 78.

130. *Prisoner for God,* pp. 85–86.

131. *Prisoner for God,* pp. 95–96.

132. *Prisoner for God,* p. 102.

133. *Prisoner for God,* pp. 110–111.

134. *Prisoner for God,* p. 112.

135. *Prisoner for God,* p. 113.

136. *Prisoner for God,* pp. 162–163.

137. *Prisoner for God,* p. 164.
138. *Prisoner for God,* pp. 165–167.
139. *Prisoner for God,* p. 169.
140. *Prisoner for God,* p. 175.
141. *Prisoner for God,* pp. 176–177.
142. *Prisoner for God,* p. 227.
143. *Prisoner for God,* p. 228.
144. *Prisoner for God,* pp. 241, 243.
145. *Prisoner for God,* p. 243.

Chapter VI: DOM HELDER CAMARA

1. José de Broucher, *Dom Helder Camara: The Violence of a Peacemaker* (Maryknoll, NY: Orbis Books, 1970), p. 5.
2. *The Church and Colonialism* (Denville, New Jersey: Dimension Books, 1969), pp. 5–6.
3. *The Church and Colonialism,* p. 6.
4. *The Church and Colonialism,* p. 12.
5. *The Church and Colonialism,* pp. 7–8.
6. *Revolution Through Peace* (New York: Harper and Row, 1971), p. 8.
7. *Revolution Through Peace,* p. 30.
8. *Revolution Through Peace,* p. 32.
9. *Revolution Through Peace,* p. 37.
10. *Charismatic Renewal and Social Action: A Dialogue* (Ann Arbor: Servant Books, 1979), p. 3.
11. *Charismatic Renewal and Social Action,* p. 76.
12. *Charismatic Renewal and Social Action,* p. 16.
13. *Charismatic Renewal and Social Action,* p. 17.
14. *Charismatic Renewal and Social Action,* p. 18.
15. *Charismatic Renewal and Social Action,* p. 19.
16. *The Conversions of a Bishop* (Glasgow: Collins, 1979), p. 21.
17. *The Conversions of a Bishop,* p. 85.
18. *Charismatic Renewal and Social Action,* p. 48.
19. *The Conversions of a Bishop,* pp. 85–86.
20. *The Conversions of a Bishop,* p. 214.
21. *Through the Gospel with Dom Helder Camara* (Maryknoll, NY: Orbis Books, 1986), p. 77.
22. *Charismatic Renewal and Social Action,* pp. 56–57.
23. *Through the Gospel,* pp. 5–6.

24. *The Desert Is Fertile* (Maryknoll, NY: Orbis Books, 1974), pp. 13–14.
25. *The Conversions of a Bishop*, p. 56.
26. *The Desert Is Fertile*, p. 41.
27. *Hoping Against All Hope* (Maryknoll, NY: Orbis Books, 1984), p. 62.
28. *Charismatic Renewal and Social Action*, p. 56.
29. *Through the Gospel*, pp. 29–30.
30. *Charismatic Renewal and Social Action*, p. 55.
31. *Through the Gospel*, p. 44.
32. *Revolution Through Peace*, p. 5.
33. *The Conversions of a Bishop*, p. 148.
34. *Hoping Against All Hope*, p. 32.
35. *Hoping Against All Hope*, p. 77.
36. *Through the Gospel*, p. 131.
37. *The Conversions of a Bishop*, p. 196.
38. *The Conversions of a Bishop*, p. 186.
39. *Through the Gospel*, p. 95.
40. *The Desert Is Fertile*, p. 17.
41. *Through the Gospel*, p. 27.
42. *Hoping Against All Hope*, pp. 27–28. The same story is told in *Charismatic Renewal and Social Action*, pp. 77–78, with the woman's name spelled Annunciade.
43. *The Conversions of a Bishop*, p. 42.
44. *The Conversions of a Bishop*, p. 86.
45. *The Conversions of a Bishop*, p. 122.
46. *The Conversions of a Bishop*, pp. 144–145.
47. *The Conversions of a Bishop*, p. 182.
48. *The Conversions of a Bishop*, p. 62.
49. *The Conversions of a Bishop*, p. 117.
50. *The Desert Is Fertile*, pp. 2–3.
51. *The Desert Is Fertile*, p. 46.
52. *The Desert Is Fertile*, p. 48.
53. *The Conversions of a Bishop*, p. 119.
54. *The Conversions of a Bishop*, p. 85.
55. *The Conversions of a Bishop*, pp. 177–178.
56. *The Conversions of a Bishop*, p. 181.
57. *The Conversions of a Bishop*, p. 199.
58. *The Conversions of a Bishop*, p. 179.
59. *The Conversions of a Bishop*, p. 97.

60. *The Conversions of a Bishop,* pp. 84–85.
61. *Through the Gospel,* p. 88.
62. *The Conversions of a Bishop,* p. 185.
63. *Through the Gospel,* p. 39.
64. *Through the Gospel,* p. 22.
65. *Charismatic Renewal and Social Action,* p. 14.
66. *Through the Gospel,* p. 31.
67. *Through the Gospel,* p. 68.
68. *The Desert Is Fertile,* pp. 8–9.
69. *The Desert Is Fertile,* p. 17.
70. *The Desert Is Fertile,* p. 38.
71. *Charismatic Renewal and Social Action,* p. 45.
72. *Hoping Against All Hope,* p. 4. See also *The Desert Is Fertile,* p. 10.
73. *Hoping Against All Hope,* p. 6.
74. *Hoping Against All Hope,* p. 74.
75. *Through the Gospel,* p. 5.
76. *Charismatic Renewal and Social Action,* p. 46.
77. *Through the Gospel,* p. 91.
78. *Through the Gospel,* p. 92.
79. *Through the Gospel,* p. 5.
80. *Through the Gospel,* p. 92.
81. *Through the Gospel,* p. 10.
82. *Through the Gospel,* p. 44.
83. *Through the Gospel,* p. 56.
84. *Through the Gospel,* p. 116.
85. *The Conversions of a Bishop,* p. 121.
86. *The Church and Colonialism,* p. 6.
87. *Hoping Against All Hope,* p. 3.
88. *Through the Gospel,* p. 144.
89. *Through the Gospel,* p. 91.
90. *Through the Gospel,* p. 138.
91. *The Conversions of a Bishop,* p. 107.
92. *The Conversions of a Bishop,* p. 92.
93. *Through the Gospel,* p. 35.
94. *The Conversions of a Bishop,* p. 82.
95. *Through the Gospel,* p. 13.
96. *Through the Gospel,* p. 13.
97. *Through the Gospel,* p. 80.
98. *The Conversions of a Bishop,* pp. 122–123.
99. *Charismatic Renewal and Social Action,* p. 80.

100. *Charismatic Renewal and Social Action,* p. 132.
101. *Hoping Against All Hope,* pp. 20–21.
102. *Hoping Against All Hope,* p. 19.
103. *Hoping Against All Hope,* p. 16.
104. *The Desert Is Fertile,* p. 34.
105. *Hoping Against All Hope,* p. 79.
106. *The Desert Is Fertile,* p. 5.
107. *The Desert Is Fertile,* p. 9.
108. *The Desert Is Fertile,* p. 68.
109. *The Desert Is Fertile,* p. 68.
110. *The Desert Is Fertile,* p. 43.